6/74

D0870981

Bonsai

PLATE 1: Tea ceremony room in the Daitokuji Monastery, Kyoto, Japan, dating from the Momoyama period (1574-1602 A.D.). The single hanging scroll in the raised alcove (*tokonomo*) is typical of the decoration of this type of room. On the floor are the implements used in the tea ceremony, and sunk in it is the fire box with the iron kettle for boiling water.

Bonsai

Dwarf Trees in the Japanese Mode

With drawings and photographs

PHYLLIS ARGALL

The Citadel Press   Secaucus, N. J.

First paperbound printing, 1974
Copyright © 1964 by Phyllis Argall Wills
All rights reserved
Published by Citadel Press
A division of Lyle Stuart, Inc.
120 Enterprise Ave., Secaucus, N.J. 07094
In Canada: George J. McLeod Limited
73 Bathurst St., Toronto 2B, Ontario
Manufactured in the United States of America
ISBN 0-8065-0423-4

Originally published as *Dwarf Trees in the Japanese Mode*

To my husband
who lived through it
and my son
who is tactfully unsurprised
at anything his mother does

Acknowledgments

To that anonymous member of the Nippon Bunka Shinkokai (Japan Cultural Society) of Tokyo, Japan, who, with nothing but written descriptions to go on, found and photographed, with meticulous exactitude, the *bon-sai, bon-kei,* and other objects I wanted as illustrations;

To Dr. James N. Freeman and Dr. Charles E. Dickinson, of the Department of Agriculture of Lincoln University, Jefferson City, Mo., for their help in translating Japanese plants, products and growing conditions, into those appropriate to the United States;

And, finally, to my good friend Carolyn Stagg, who never gave up and would not let me give up either.

Notes:

ILLUSTRATIONS:

All photos, are, as noted, supplied by the Nippon Bunka Shinkokai (Japan Cultural Society, Tokyo, Japan) for this volume.

Ink sketches are the author's, after Japanese original.

HAIKU translations:

Translations of the Japanese *haiku* (17-syllable verse) used in chapters 2, 11, 13 and 15, are my own.

LEGEND (Chap. 16)

The legend of the dwarf trees is re-told from the Japanese version told me by a very old Japanese lady who made a hobby of collecting little-known legends and stories.

List of Illustrations

Contents

Bonsai

. . . That makes simplicity a grace.
—BEN JONSON

What Is a Dwarf Tree?

WHAT is a dwarf tree? Obviously, one would suppose, a tree which through some accident of nature never attains its full growth, but remains always a miniature specimen of its kind.

Such is the literal sense of the phrase. But to the dwarf tree devotee, this is the merest shadow, a simulacrum "seen through a glass darkly." The dwarf tree as understood by the Japanese, who, having borrowed the idea from the Chinese, perfected, refined and made it peculiarly their own, is a work of art, a tiny replica of nature, achieved only by devoted care and supreme patience.

The Japanese keeps his tree tiny, ethereal, exquisite, for the same reason and in much the same way as the ancient Chinese bound his women's feet and the Russian Imperial Ballet laced its little girls into steel corsets. He binds it. And, with the trees, the result is perfection.

The dwarf tree of the Japanese mode may be a minuscule, no more than a foot high, displaying all the characteristics of a forest giant; gnarled branches tortured by the winds of a century; moss-laden roots clinging precariously to inhospitable rock, until it is hard to tell whether the tree keeps the rock from being hurled into the abyss or the rock anchors the tree against the precipice.

It may be a trunk not so long as one's arm, seamed and scarred with infinite age, twisted by storms; yet bearing on its cascading branches the drift of pink, or white, or lavender or yellow blossoms that tell the miracle of spring and rebirth.

On the other hand, it may be a trunk a bare six inches in length but thick as a muscular man's wrist, resting on a tall support; at one end, queer, snake-like branches bearing tufts of glistening dark needles; at the other, strangely elongated roots, stretching, writhing toward the soil three feet below, in odd, exaggeratedly theatrical mime of the tree beside the waterfall, from whose roots recurrent flooding torrents have washed the soil until it hangs precariously in mid-air.

If the Japanese are masters of miniature, they are likewise masters of simplicity. Their art is either very small or very

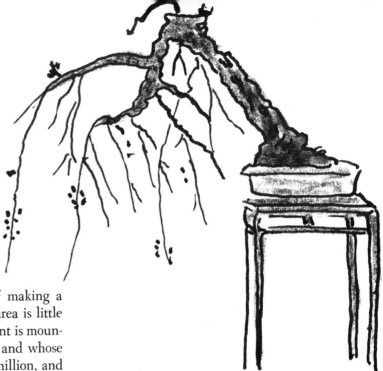

simple. Probably this results from the impulse of making a virtue of necessity. Certainly, in a country whose area is little more than 142,000 square miles, of which 75 per cent is mountain and approximately only 12 per cent is arable, and whose population, estimated in the 1880's, as around 30 million, and is 96 million today, there has never been much opportunity for great size or great wealth. The fact that farms are measured

PLATE 2: Single tree, leaning.

by *tsubo* (a 6 by 6 foot square) and rooms by *tatami* mats (3 by 6 feet, or a half-tsubo) is indicative of the scale on which the people must live. There is neither room nor material to waste.

Whether for that reason or any other, the Japanese has raised the appreciation of the small and unostentatious almost to the level of a cult, going even beyond the Aristotelian "nothing too much" to an ideal of, apparently, "barely enough."

True, the tourist recently returned from Japan will ask, "What about the Great Buddha of Kamakura, the multi-colored glories of Nikko, the silk and brocade *geisha*?" unaware that these, though certainly the most spectacular, are on that account alone considered by the Japanese themselves as not the finest examples of their art and beauty. In fact, they are rather apt to decry the gaudy mausolea of the Tokugawas, the opulent gold Kinkakuji and silver-leaf Ginkakuji, as striking but innately tasteless examples of typical *nouveau riche* flamboyance. Of far greater beauty in Japanese eyes are the cryptomeria-log Grand Shrine of Ise, the plain wood Kiyomizu temple of Kyoto, the soaring Greek austerity of the great *torii*. One of the most celebrated gardens in Japan is an expanse of white sand, raked daily into wave-like patterns.

In all their art, the Japanese would rather suggest than state. Their classical poetic form is the 17-syllable *haiku,* so condensed and allusive that a single poem may serve as the subject of an evening's contemplation. Their choicest paintings are not great canvasses glowing with the colors of a Titian or the tortured detail of a Greco, but a narrow strip of silk with a single delicate flower, or perhaps a dragon fly, or a mountain crest seen vaguely through a mist.

In the theatre, too, there is a world of difference between the brilliant, gaudy and exciting *Kabuki* of popular taste and the quiet, highly stylized *Noh* with its solitary dancer, wooden masked and clothed in dim silk, moving in stiff, symbolic, ritually controlled posture before a dull gold screen.

Even in domestic architecture, the Japanese has evolved a perfection of understatement; of natural wood, only rarely lacquered black; of plaster, quiet gray or dim green or pale ivory; of matted floors whose white may sometimes have a pale green or gold sheen; of quiet rooms furnished with a few cushions of dark silk, the only decoration a vase of flowers, a single picture, perhaps an oddly shaped rock. Their very clothes demonstrate the same characteristics. Vivid colors are the prerogatives of tiny girls, brides, geisha—and tourists. For himself or herself, the adult Japanese prefers black, dull brown or gray silks, their richness in the subtleties of hand weaving.

Yet with all this reserve and reticence, this lack of superficial color, there is a certain sophisticated and delicate wit. The Japanese sobriety can be decidedly a sort of tongue-in-cheek affair. The black or midnight blue ceremonial kimono of the lady, ornamented with nothing but a spray of flowers across one corner of the skirt, may, in moving, reveal a tantalizing glimpse of scarlet silk petticoat. The gentleman, severely austere in his formal skirt of stiff dark silk will sport on his tobacco pouch a *netsuke* (tiny ivory bead and fob) of uninhibited bawdiness, as broad in nature as it is exquisite in craftsmanship. (Whole books have been and still could be written on these wonderful little *netsuke*). And his *haori* may be lined with hand blocked printed silk whose subject matter is strikingly at variance with its sombre hues.

In the Japanese way of life, the utmost in beauty, that inward beauty of mind disciplined through philosophy, expressed in the outward grace of ritually prescribed gesture perfected through practice, is the tea ceremony. This is as far as the East is from the West, from the occidental "tea party," with its massive sterling service, its chink of fine china drowned in the parrot-clatter of voices. To the uninitiated, the Japanese ceremony is apt to appear as nothing but a long-drawn-out process of serving a cup of somewhat unappetising, lukewarm, soupy tea to a couple of friends. The equipment is so sparse that a single cup, of thick, handcrafted pottery, is made to serve for all, carefully (and ritualistically) rinsed between servings. Water is boiled in an iron pot over an open charcoal fire, ladled with a bamboo dipper; the tea measured with a bamboo spoon from a pottery or pewter container. The room (Plate 1) itself is small, overlooking a green, secluded garden, and everything about it is equally quiet and unostentatious, though the host may, being pressed, confess that yes, the cup is some six centuries old, and worth a fortune; and the bamboo spoon is beyond price, having been used by one of the great Tea Masters. He may also admit, upon interrogation by the blunt foreigner, that the three adornments of the room, the hanging scroll, the incense burner, and the dwarf tree, are family heirlooms, and therefore to him invaluable.

(Incidentally, the foreigner will do well to express praise up to, but not beyond, the limits of polite and informed ap-

Plate 2a: Single tree, upright, planted in a flat container to suggest a plain.

preciation. Otherwise the host must, in courtesy bound, make a gift of the admired object. A friend of the writer had the experience once of receiving as a gift a pair of exquisite miniature facsimiles of the lanterns of the Grand Shrine of Ise, which he had admired extravagantly, to discover that they had been heirlooms in his host's family for some 500 years!)

And if it seems a long way from dwarf trees to the tea ceremony, it is, in actual fact, but a short one; for in Japanese philosophy, psychology, art and convention, they are very closely linked. The one can hardly be appreciated without at least some slight knowledge of the other.

Not without art, but yet to nature true.
—CHARLES CHURCHILL: "The Rosciad"

2*

Classifications of Dwarf Trees

THE Japanese love for the dwarf tree is symbolic of yet another emotional characteristic, their innate love of nature; not so much of wild and uninhibited nature, but of those calmer aspects which lend themselves to the contemplative mood. A rocky, storm-lashed sea coast is less beloved than a quiet tree-shadowed lake. The serene peak of Fuji, snow-encrusted, cloud-girt, observed through the blossoming cherry bough; the immaculate moon full-orbed against the dark sky; pines fringing a pale sanded beach; the silvery tassels of the *susuki* bent by the autumn breeze; fireflies winking above the Kamo river; the sound of a frog in a quiet pond*; these are the manifestations the Japanese most deeply appreciates.

* One of the most famous and best-loved poems in the Japanese language is the 17-syllable *haiku* of the poet Basho (1644-1694): Furuike ya/Kawazu tobikomu/Mizu no oto—literally translated: "An ancient pond; a frog leaping; the sound of water."

Hence the Japanese garden; not a stretch of grass lawn sprinkled with flower beds and banked with flowering shrubs, but a copy of nature, even if a highly civilized, conventionalized, not to say standardized copy—nature with its hair combed and its shoes shined. Trees moss-rooted; magnificent uncut stones; tiny waterfalls tumbling down a man-made precipice into an artfully casual lake complete with islets; all in careful scale, so planned that the eye is carried back and back and back, until a landscape covering barely an acre gives one a sense of unlimited horizons. However tiny a plot the Japanese has at his disposal, in however unideal a location, he must have a garden. The writer remembers one such, in pre-war Tokyo. The site was the entranceway to a back-street bar. Less than two feet wide, certainly not five feet long, it was but a hedge of growing bamboo, a little pine, a tiny pebble path, tucked into the dead-end alley; yet as one looked, the neon-lighted bar, the street lamps, the roaring Ginza a scant block away faded into the quiet stars and soughing wind of the forest.

The modern American architectural slogan of "bringing the outdoors in" is only a variation of what the Japanese has been doing for hundreds of years. More accurately, the Japanese *in*doors is *out*. To sit in a Japanese home on a hot summer night, the doors standing open to the garden, the room bare of the distracting planes and angles of chairs and tables, the moonlit black and white of floors blends with the delicate shadows of trees and stones. An even more perfect aesthetic delight is the same scene in winter, when snow gleams white in the moonlight, trees crowned and girdled in straw against the cold, throwing deep shadows of blackness, and a candle flickering in an old stone lantern speaks of human love and companionship. But such garden viewing is only for the hardy, whose love of unearthly beauty lifts him above the mundane actuality of freezing hands and frost-tipped nose.

Lacking a garden with full-scale trees to contemplate, the Japanese turns to dwarf trees. Or even if he has a garden, he still loves his tree, as a work of art that is at the same time a dear companion. In fact, especially tiny trees, in pots merely two or three inches high, may be grown for the purpose of carrying around, much like a lady's bouquet! Thus the dwarf tree must, as has been said before, imitate nature; yet withal must somehow transcend it, with an artistic impact and impulse to quiet contemplation which nature, unchoosing of her setting and unselective of her details, generally fails to achieve to unalloyed perfection. With a philosophic disposition to look below the surface and beyond the visible, the Japanese requires of his tree, into which he puts so much loving patient artistry, that it suggest beauties and truths not immediately obvious.

Therefore, certain trees are suitable for certain occasions and seasons. According to one school of thought, there are ten types of dwarf tree. They are:

Evergreens to be admired throughout the four seasons;

Trees which are at their most beautiful when flowering in spring;

Trees bearing flowers in summer;

Trees with flowers that bloom in fall;

Trees whose winter flowering brightens and inspires in the snow;

Trees and plants whose chief beauty is in the delicate sprouting of spring foliage;

Trees to be admired in summer for their cool deep green;

Trees whose greatest beauty is their changing, glittering fall color;

Trees which bear fruit and berries in spring, summer or fall;

Trees whose chief interest is the odd or interesting shape of branches or trunk, which show to greatest advantage in winter, when bare of foliage.

While some trees may be equally lovely in two seasons, few, of course, can fittingly be displayed in all four. This, however, does not distress the Japanese. He does not believe in keeping things of even greatest beauty on constant exhibition. To do so would, for one thing, be ostentatious; for another, it would be unsuitable. A spring scene is inappropriate to fall, as Christmas holly cannot be mingled in a bouquet with June roses. A wealthy and/or aristocratic Japanese may own pictures worth hundreds or thousands of dollars, but he would never dream of crowding his walls with them, as do many of our collectors. Rather, they are kept in a vault, to be hung only a few at a time, one to a room, when the occasion or season is suitable. In like manner, he grows his extraordinary chrysanthemums in pots, in a secluded spot, to be massed in display only when their bloom reaches perfection. So also he keeps his dwarf trees out of sight, though scrupulously tended, except when they are at their best.

The list of ten types of tree is, of course, only one of the many ways of classifying them. Another method places them in categories according to the type of scene they represent. Of these there are six:

> A single tree, upright (Plate 2a) or leaning (Plate 2);
>
> Two trees apparently growing from a single trunk (Plates 3, 3a);
>
> Several trees grouped, to suggest a glade or forest (Plate 4);
>
> Trees with high exposed roots (Plate 5);
>
> Trees with roots embracing a rock (Plates 9, 9a).
>
> Trees that bend sharply down as if hanging over a cliff (Plate 11, 11a);

A man does not plant a tree for
himself; he plants it for posterity.
—DREAMTHORP: *Books and Gardens*

3

FROM all of which it will
by now be obvious that the decision to grow a dwarf tree
according to Japanese techniques is in one respect at least akin
to the state of holy matrimony: it is not by any to be enter-
prised, nor taken in hand unadvisedly, lightly or wantonly . . .
but reverently, discreetly, advisedly and soberly." In somewhat more literal vein, the opening chapter of one treatise
on the subject* is headed "Infinite patience is required in
growing dwarf plants."

Some recent advertising and publicity to the contrary,
the producing of a dwarf tree is neither easy nor quick. There
are a few short cuts but no swift successes. It requires a
minimum of three years before your miniature tree even

* "Dwarf Trees," Samuel Newsome, *Japan News Week*, Tokyo, Japan,
November 9, 1940.

Start with a Plan

begins to take on the characteristics of the true dwarf, and it is anything up to ten before it approximates the desired result. After that, each decade adds to its beauty, until the century-old gem has a fascination all its own. And if actuarial figures suggest that the present reader is hardly likely to see his own effort culminate in such perfection, he can at least take pride in the fact that he is preparing something supremely beautiful for the delight of his grandchildren and great grandchildren.

PLATE 3: Tree with divided trunk.

On the other hand, there is nothing surpassingly diffi-cult in tree dwarfing. An observing eye, a delicate hand, a few elementary tools, deep affection and eternal patience—particularly deep affection and eternal patience—are all that is required.

Dwarf tree culture need not demand even a great deal of room, and hence is a hobby well adapted to apartment dwellers. If one is willing to bypass the very earliest steps of seed and seedbed or cutting bed, and start with a well-rooted seedling already an inch or two high, then a couple of cubic feet of storage space for supplies and equipment, and a sunny window, are the chief accommodations needed.

The production of a dwarf tree begins, not with the planting of the seed or cutting of the slip, but with plans laid long before. No builder would lay a foundation or put up a beam before he knew whether the finished edifice were to be a barn or a house or a hospital. A purpose and a blueprint must precede such practical activities. The same is true of the dwarf tree. One must start with a clear concept of the desired result, for the end will dictate the beginning.

Is your tree to be an evergreen, for display, perhaps, the

year around? Is it to give a sense of peace and calm, or of struggle and indomitable courage? Is it to bloom or bear fruit? Is it to evoke a forest glade, shadowed in quietness, or will it cling precariously to a cliff overhanging some vast suggested chasm? These considerations will govern not only the kind of tree you plan to grow, but the container in which you grow it, even the table or stand on which it is to be eventually displayed.

There is no need, and in fact, considering the length of time involved, there is no purpose in hurrying to start your tree. The process of reaching a decision as to what you want to achieve can be delightful and rewarding in itself.

The enthusiast who insists that his tree be truly Japanese may want to work from Japanese plans. The Japanese themselves frequently follow sketches contained in a set of books known as *Keshi Engaden* (*The Poppy Garden*). More readily obtainable over here are reproductions of Japanese paintings or woodcuts, many delineating trees which would make excellent subjects. Or he might find a photograph of some existing dwarf tree (or, for that matter, one of the illustrations in this very volume) and reproduce a facsimile.

However, since the dwarf tree is ideally, as we have already stressed, nature in miniature (even if worked upon by art) why not start by finding a natural tree to imitate? At the risk of sounding an utter iconoclast, the writer sees no basic or incontrovertible objection to the American hobbyist growing a tree of a type and shape more native to the local scene. Indigenous American nature is neither more nor less beautiful than the exotic Japanese, only different. For another thing, the appreciation of an "American" dwarf tree would require less of an educated or informed taste on the part of the observer. The taste for a Toyokuni or even a Hiroshige woodcut is the product of a far more critical knowledge than is the appreciation of Grandma Moses or Norman Rockwell, though in origin and purpose the two types were not radically dissimilar.

Working on this basis, the dwarf tree planner will find the search for a tree to imitate a rewarding hobby in itself. On drives to the lake or seashore, rambles through meadows, orchard or forest, note the trees, the way they grow, how they hang, and the way their branches are twisted. The artistically inclined will find himself sketching trees or groups; the camera bug can collect tree portraits for later study and imitation. Even those who (like the writer) entirely lack artistic ability, can make rough sketches, enough to indicate a beauty to be recollected in tranquility. Or one may prefer to reproduce some well known scene, such as Pebble Beach or Monterey on the California coast.

Then, having chosen one's effect, one is ready to choose the tree.

The difficulty in life is the choice
—GEORGE MOORE: *The Bending of the Bough*

4

What Tree and What Style?

SINCE the type of effect desired will govern the selection of tree to be dwarfed, the choice is naturally largely subjective. However, there are certain limitations which, even though broad, the amateur will do well to consider. Some trees lend themselves to almost any type of treatment, others are by shape or nature appropriate within a narrower range. Some are definitely unsuitable for dwarfing, though the expert might find interest in experimentation even with these.

Generally speaking, trees which in nature have tall, straight trunks, with branches beginning rather high up, are best for grouping. Flower and fruit trees are most effective when grown singly, with only enough shaping to emphasize their natural lines. And trees with outsize or sparse leaves and/or disproportionately large flowers, such as the magnolia,

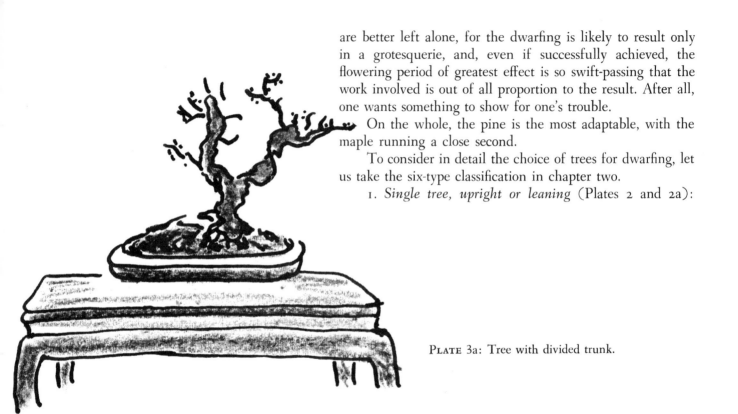

are better left alone, for the dwarfing is likely to result only in a grotesquerie, and, even if successfully achieved, the flowering period of greatest effect is so swift-passing that the work involved is out of all proportion to the result. After all, one wants something to show for one's trouble.

On the whole, the pine is the most adaptable, with the maple running a close second.

To consider in detail the choice of trees for dwarfing, let us take the six-type classification in chapter two.

1. *Single tree, upright or leaning* (Plates 2 and 2a):

PLATE 3a: Tree with divided trunk.

Dwarf Trees in the Japanese Mode

This is the simplest type, and is suitable for almost any tree; with the exception that a tree with a trunk relatively tall in proportion to the length or density of branch is the most rewarding as far as appearance is concerned. The pine and maple are popular, and so are the spruce and juniper. However, since the first two of these in particular are amenable to the utmost in imaginative treatment, the grower will probably want to leave them for one of the other categories. The flower and fruit trees are particularly appropriate for single growing. Plum and cherry are the most popular among the Japanese, with peach running a close third, but the orange, particularly the tiny kumquat, is also seen. Here in the United States, there is no reason why the apple also should not be dwarfed, and, conceivably, even the mulberry. The writer must admit to never having seen a dwarf mulberry; however, with its rough trunk and spreading branches, it might be effective. Probably the reason the Japanese do not use it is that to them it is a "working" shrub, with the one specific duty of providing food for silkworms.

Nor need the word "upright" imply any lack of interest in the trunk. It may be curiously gnarled, twisted vertically, seamed and rugged, exemplifying the strength to stand and endure against decades of storm and buffeting.

Fruit trees, especially those whose branches may be trained to cascade, such as the plum or cherry, are suitable also for a single leaning tree. Note, however, there is a distinction between the "leaning tree" of category 1, and the "cliff hanger" of category 5.

2. *Two trees out of a single trunk* (Plate 3): Here again choice of species is wide. The Japanese still prefer pine, maple, cherry or plum. An elm might be used, even an oak. However, one of the best ways to choose your subject is to study nature herself, to see what she does.

3. *Several trees grouped, to suggest a glade or forest* (Plate 4): Obviously, where five or more trees are to be grouped in one small container, they cannot be types with wide, spreading branches. (Incidentally, the reason for the choice of five is due to the fact that the Japanese would never put four in one arrangement. The word for "four" is identical in sound with that for "death" and is therefore unlucky. Three trees could hardly suggest a glade, so the minimum number must be five.) Nor are flowering trees suitable, for the bunch-

ing of them would prevent the showing of their full beauty. The elm is the most popular Japanese tree for this treatment, but the silver birch, growing from a mossy "plain" would be singularly exquisite. Poplar might be experimented with, and even oak would not be entirely unsuitable, though the effect might be somewhat massive.

The matter of size and style of container for displaying the dwarf trees will be taken up in more detail later, but a word on the subject might be appropriate with this particular classification. The Japanese has a fondness for off-center effects, and his dwarf tree is as likely to be to one side of the container as in the center. This is particularly true with the "forest-suggesting" arrangement. The line or group of trees must always be towards one end and at the far side of a shallow, oblong dish. The nearer side and the other end are then covered in moss or, perhaps, sand, so that the eye is carried from the edge, across a plain to the trees in the distance. Incredible as it may sound, even in so small a confine, a sense of space is achieved, the effect being that of looking across a meadow or prairie to a bluff of trees on the horizon. Anyone who has travelled across the plains of western Kansas will know the buoyant promise of rest and refreshment offered by a far-off group of trees.

4. *Trees with high exposed roots* (Plate 5): This particular formation is a *tour de force*, quite definitely "caviar to the general." A mannered freak, it is not everybody's dish. One cannot even claim that it is close to nature. The Japanese themselves admire it as an oddity, a little original relaxation. For this type, the grower had better confine his efforts to the tree used by the Japanese, which is the red or black pine.

5. *Trees that bend sharply down, as if hanging over a cliff* (Plates 11 and 11a): This tree is distinguished from Type 2 by effect to be produced, which in turn governs the species of tree that may be used. Any tree can be blown by prevailing winds until it leans, rather than stands upright. But not all trees can cling precariously to a cliff with an unconquerable will to live. Hence the wild, rather than the domesticated types are best. Trees favored by the Japanese for this treatment are the conifers, the maple, and the azalea.

6. *Trees with roots embracing a rock* (Plates 9 and 9a): Trees which have a natural spread of branch and therefore heavy spreading roots, are best for this arrangement. The

Japanese prefer the pine, which is found in almost any circumstances and conditions, and seems amenable to almost any treatment, and the almost equally adaptable maple. The former is striking throughout the year. The latter is particularly lovely in spring and fall, when the tender green of the new leaves, or the blazing scarlet and gold of the passing year contrast with the aged gnarled roots and dark stone. However, the cherry and plum are also sometimes used, and the apple and oak almost certainly could be. Again, the azalea is popular.

Before making a final choice of type of tree and effect, there are a few generalizations the beginner should consider.

One of these is speed of growth. The Japanese is more or less oblivious to this consideration. After all, he feels, if his tree cannot be brought to perfection during his lifetime, a son or even grandson may safely be trusted to carry on the work. The American will want to see results somewhat more speedily. So the beginner is advised to undertake the dwarfing of a species which grows reasonably swiftly. Among the flower-and-fruit trees, the orange is probably one of the quickest to develop, and the plum one of the slowest. According to a Japanese proverb, it takes eighteen years for a plum to bloom,

PLATE 4: Several trees grouped, to suggest a glade or forest.

though there are, fortunately, some shortcuts allowable in the production of dwarf trees, which will be discussed in a later chapter.

The second feature to consider is the relative number of branches natural to the species of tree. Some trees produce them in profusion, at all angles, without set scheme or direction; others are positively niggardly; whereas yet others, though reasonably luxuriant, doggedly produce straight, parallel branches with the unimaginative regularity of a ladder. Of the three types, the first is naturally the simplest for the cultivator to train in the effect he desires. He is reasonably sure of finding a branch where he wants it, malleable enough to be trained according to plan.

Thirdly—and most practically—the tree should be tough; no neurotic hypochrondriac that bruises at a glance, that wilts if its water is not measured to the exact tenth of a cubic centimeter, or dies if a breath of cool (or warm) air hits it unexpectedly. Dwarfing inevitably involves handling, wiring, trimming, of both roots and branches, and only a reasonably sturdy tree can stand it. The beginner in particular is advised to choose his tree with an eye to its probable stamina.

. . . little jars
For you to take and put upon a shelf.
Their shapes are quaint and beautiful,
And they have many pleasant colors and lustres.
—AMY LOWELL: "A Gift"

5

Choice of a Container

HAVING selected the kind of tree to be dwarfed and decided on the effect ultimately to be achieved, the next matter which must be considered is the container, or pot, in which it will be placed. Of course, it may be some time before a container is needed, especially if the seed, seedling, or clipping is to be started in a seed bed. But since the grower who really loves his tree will insist on finding exactly the right container for it, the search may take quite a while.

The main point to remember is that the two elements, tree and pot, form a single unit. One cannot use just "any old pot" because it happens to be handy, or even a beautiful one because it is a choice specimen of its kind and worthy of display. There is a mutual interdependence between tree and container, and form, color, style and character must combine in one integral work of art. Lack of harmony in any of these particulars will spoil the finest tree or the most expensive container.

Hence the time for matching tree and container is at the early planning stage. Indeed, one may even start with the container rather than the tree. If one is lucky enough to find a particularly choice container which cries aloud for a tree of a certain type or style of dwarfing, the young tree may be chosen and shaped to suit it.

The reader will observe that the word "container" is used here in preference to the more usual "pot." This is because the word "pot" is likely to bring to mind something along the lines of our flower pot, round, and considerably deeper than it is wide. Whereas, though the Japanese grower does sometimes use a pot for his tree, he is even more likely to choose a tray-shaped container with length and width far exceeding the depth.

Technically speaking, the Japanese purist divides the art of tree dwarfing into two categories, according to the type of container: *bon-sai,* or "tray cultivation" and *hachi uye* or "pot planted." However, today the one word *bon-sai* is popularly used for both types.

And, though we have been referring to the "container" in the singular, in practice the grower will find that as the tree develops, he will need a whole series of containers, each somewhat, but not much, larger than the one before it. He may also wish to use both "growing" containers and "exhibition" containers. These, naturally, must be similar in size and shape, or the roots will be damaged, possibly seriously, in transferring from one to the other. And since the little tree will be loved and admired even in its early years of training, the growing pots themselves will be selected with an eye to material, color and style.

An additional reason for beginning the search early, is that a container must have certain structural qualities if the tree is to do well in it. If the hobbyist is fortunate enough (or rich enough) to obtain a genuine Oriental antique made for the exhibition of dwarf trees, these structural requirements will probably have been built in. This is not always true of the newer ones, American or Oriental. However, many of the defects can be overcome with a little careful reconstruction work.

Fortunately, this searching for and preparation of containers, all except the first one, can be carried on during those

PLATE 5: Pine with high, exposed roots. Note "crutch" in center which supports the short, thin trunk. The long snake-like branches, with a few tufts of needles, and the twisted roots are characteristic of this peculiar type of tree.

somewhat dull periods when the tiny trees are doing nothing but growing slowly. It will help beguile the tedium; and—who knows—it may even lead to the taking up of a parallel or subsidiary hobby, that of the study of Japanese, Korean and Chinese pottery!

The choice of container for the dwarf tree depends ultimately, of course, on the aesthetic perception of the grower and his appreciation of line, balance and color. But a few generalizations may be made. For the sake of convenience, the containers will be considered under the two headings of *Form* and *Color*. Construction will be discussed in the next chapter.

FORM

Obviously, the broadest categories into which containers may be divided according to form are: round, oval, or polygonal. But this is only the beginning. The round or oval types may be deep and flat-bottomed, like our flower-pot; large-surfaced and shallow as a tray; or a wide bowl, shallow in proportion to its diameter, with a relatively small base. And with any of these styles, the base may either rest directly on the table, or be supported on tiny feet.

The polygonal containers are even more various. They may be square, oblong, six or eight-sided, diamond or counter-diamond (diamond with the corners cut in). They may be extremely shallow or relatively deep, though, generally speaking, with the polygonal containers, the surface area is large in proportion to the depth. Some may have fluted or "pie crust" edges.

Occasionally one finds somewhat odd containers, shaped like a leaf, a melon, or a gourd. These, however, are not in the best conservative tradition, and are considered too spectacular to be in perfect taste.

And, rather in a class by themselves, are the extremely deep, narrow pots, more like a vase than a flower pot, used with the drooping-branch style of tree. These may be either round or polygonal. Whether the grower decides to use a tray or a pot will depend in large part on the effect he wishes to produce.

Within somewhat broad limits, a dwarf tree whose main interest is in the roots (Plates 9, 9a) or both root and branches, looks best in a shallow container, which emphasizes the root by distracting as little attention as possible to itself. It also suggests the root rising far above the flat earth. An exception to this rule is made, however, in the case of the high, exposed root (Plate 5) which requires a pot with relatively small surface area but of sufficient depth to give secure anchorage to the necessary wooden support.

A tree with a heavy, thick or twisted trunk may be placed in a relatively deep pot, since such trees need a heavy growth of root to support them. But where a tree with a particularly heavy trunk is planned to give an impression of space and distance, an oval or oblong deep tray may be used, the large surface area giving the sense of space, and the depth providing plenty of stability.

In some cases, of course, there is no question whatever as to whether a shallow tray or deep pot should be used. A group suggestive of a forest glade must be planted in a shallow dish, preferably oblong. A deep pot with little surface area would spoil the balance and proportion; for the illusion of space and distance can be achieved only by horizontal lines.

On the other hand, a tree with long branches drooping at an angle as if hanging from a cliff or over a wall is generally·planted in a tall, slim pot (Plate 11a), which permits the branches to hang free above the table. The tall pot is,

however, by no means an invariable rule. At times a shallow
bowl is used, in which case the tree must be displayed on a
tall stand, little larger in diameter than the bowl itself.

COLOR

Proportion of depth to surface area, the matter of round
or polygonal, are by no means the only factors to be considered in the selection of the perfect container for the dwarf
tree. Color of pottery and glaze, the type and amount of
decoration, must be chosen with an eye to unity of impression,
so that the container will both support and reflect the beauty
of the tree planted therein.

The dwarf tree owner who wishes to boast of the ex-
trinsic value as well as intrinsic beauty of his exhibit may, if
he likes, seek out one of the ancient, and fabulously expensive,
Chinese, Korean or Japanese containers still in existence; and
discourse with erudition on the relative beauties and appropri-
ateness of Old Seto, Old Bizen, Old Satsuma, Shinraku,
Korai, Shidei, and other types.

But such rich and fastidious elegance is by no means
essential. Beautiful effects are achieved with quite inexpen-

sive, modern containers. And in these days of do-it-yourself home ceramic manufacture, the hobbyist might enjoy making his own container, or getting a friend to make one for him.

Containers are usually of pottery, sometimes, though more rarely, of porcelain. The clay may be left unglazed, in its original color, white, gray, black, or the various shades of brown. It may have an all-over colored glaze, either glossy or dull. Or a two-tone effect may be achieved, either by a single glaze "dribbled" over the basic clay, so that some of it remains uncovered, or an overglaze "dribbled" over an underglaze. The ultimate effect should always be one of unforced naturalness, of lack of artifice.

Sometimes, especially in the case of the very deep pot of natural unglazed clay, one finds a design, either incised or in relief. This is usually somewhat formal and geometric in effect, but even here the emphasis is on naturalness. There must be no machine-age regularity or mathematical precision.

Japanese dwarf tree specialists recognize five official colors for containers: white, red, black, blue-green, and yellow. To these popular practice adds lavender, coral, lapis, gray, and intermediate shades.

Naturally, the type of tree and the color of the foliage, flowers or blossoms determine the color and shade of the container. Here are a few generally recognized as appropriate and acceptable:

Evergreens, such as pines, junipers and others: containers having a suggestion of green-grey, or lavender; or brown; browns, and dark greens, either by themselves or in combination.

Flowers: Containers to match or contrast with the flowers. Thus white plums may look well in black pots, and red plums in white pots; a pink-flowering peach in a white pot; a flowering quince in a cream pot.

Maples and other trees remarkable for the brilliance of their fall foliage: white, green, cream, or blue-green containers.

The use of white sand or moss to cover the earth around the tree roots and take away the "naked" look may also influence, and be influenced by, the color of the container. Some dwarf tree artists are particularly fond of the contrast of pure, sparkling white sand spread around the base of a tree in a dark-green container; whereas a white or cream container will be used if the roots are moss-covered. Others

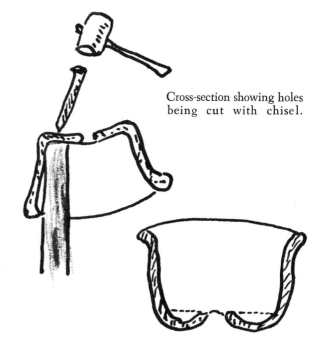

Cross-section showing holes being cut with chisel.

Cross-section of poorly drained pot with depressions filled in with clay.

PLATE 6: Two methods of improving drainage in a pot.

feel there is too much contrast in the former combination, and that the shining white breaks the unity of shading of container, root, and tree. Such matters are for the individual to decide for himself. He may want to experiment, taking into consideration his own container and his own individual tree.

Oh, the little more, and how much it is!
And the little less, and what worlds away!
   —BROWNING: "By the Fireside".

6

Structural Requirements
of the Container

IMPORTANT though the outside of the container may be from an aesthetic point of view, the inside structural qualities are of quite as much, if not more, concern to the dwarf tree grower, for on these may depend the health and development of his pet.

A basic necessity in a dwarf tree container is good drainage. This is, of course, desirable in any flower or plant pot, but is doubly important for dwarf trees. As the roots of the growing tree develop, they may at last actually fill the container. Then, if there are any places where water may stand without draining off, the roots become saturated and gradually rot, killing, or at best seriously harming, the plant. And even though the roots themselves may not come in contact with the standing moisture, the earth will sour and become unhealthy.

Many containers, whether pot or dish type, will have

drainage holes already provided. Containers which are appreciably longer than they are wide should have holes near each end. For round pots, a single hole in the center is sufficient, but its size should be commensurate with that of the pot. In addition to this, the container should be carefully examined to see that no portion of the inside surface is lower than the lip of the drainage hole. An older container is probably satisfactory in this respect, or it would not have been used. New ones may frequently be defective. Even the very expensive, one-of-a-kind item handcrafted by an artist may have been formed with more attention to outside beauty than inside efficiency, and so should be examined warily.

Fortunately, there are ways of improving the internal structural qualities of a container without affecting the outside.

One of these methods is to drill or chisel an extra hole, or holes, in the lowest part of the pot. An emory wheel may be used, and the writer has had some success with an ordinary brace and bit and small ($\frac{1}{16}$ to $\frac{1}{8}$ inches) drill, though some chipping resulted. The Japanese often use a chisel and mallet (Plate 8), but this technique should be resorted to only with the cheapest pots, for despite extreme care, some breakage is almost inevitable. In both methods, the pot should be inverted over a post or some firm object which will not "give," and which distributes the pressure rather than permitting it to be concentrated at one point.

The most satisfactory, certainly the safest, way of dealing with the situation is to fill in the depressed portions of the container (Plate 6). Cement is excellent. Very little is needed, for a cupfull mixed with sand goes a long way, and the writer has found that suppliers of building materials can be very helpful and cooperative in "liberating" a small quantity from a split sack. Actually, any substance that may be easily molded, yet holds its shape, is satisfactory. When working with a container to be used only temporarily, the writer has used paraffin wax, and even children's plastic modelling clay. Both of these substances can be removed easily without damage to the container, and are suitable, for instance, for exhibition containers which the owner may wish to put to other purposes later.

If containers of very porous material, notably unglazed red clay, are used, less attention need be paid to drainage potential, as the water is absorbed and eventually evaporates. However, some method of efficient drainage, which allows the water actually to escape from the container, is absolutely essential. The practice often employed with house plants in this country, of putting a layer of coarse gravel in the bottom of an undrained, jardiniere-type pot, is definitely unsafe for dwarf trees, since, as has been pointed out earlier, there is danger of the water standing and souring.

On the other hand, it is necessary also to prevent soil from being drained out with the water, and hence the holes must be covered. Flat materials which fit too closely to the bottom of the container and so form a seal, are not advisable. A curved pottery shard is good, or a flat stone if tilted on edge (Plate 7); or fine wire or plastic screening may be fitted over the inside bottom surface of the container.

While the type of soil used for the actual planting will depend on the species of tree (see chart, Chapter 7) it is appropriate here to mention the bottom layers, since these are concerned with the drainage problem. Whatever soil the individual tree may require for growing, the bottom of the container should be covered with a layer of some coarse material through which excess moisture may seep easily. Better still are two or three layers of gradually decreasing coarseness. The first, about half an inch in depth, may be of gravel, the size of a navy bean. Above this is a layer of finer gravel or very coarse earth particles, and, covering this, a thin layer of coarse sand. The three layers are optional, but there should be at least two between the bottom of the container and the growing soil itself.

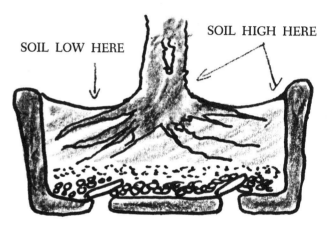

SOIL LOW HERE

SOIL HIGH HERE

PLATE 7: Cross-section of dwarf tree planted in a container, showing drainage holes and arrangement of soil for good drainage.

Structural Requirements of the Container · 45 ·

7

Starting the Tree

Gardener, you behold
New beginnings and new shoots.
—ROBERT GRAVES: "Marigolds"

So NOW, having decided upon the type of trees to be dwarfed and the effect to be achieved, which considerations are interdependent; and having chosen, or being in process of choosing, a container, which itself is again an integral part of the whole project— we are ready to look for our tree.

There are traditionally five ways of starting a dwarf tree, each with its innate advantages and disadvantages; each with its group of devotees among Japanese growers. These five accepted methods are:

1. From a wild, or natural, seedling
2. From a cutting or slip
3. By layering
4. By a graft
5. From seed

Greatly prized by the Japanese is the dwarfed Chinese

juniper (juniperus chinensis), alternatively known as Sargent's juniper, developed from a wild seedling. The juniper lends itself particularly well to the art of dwarfing, for the miniature is startlingly like its life-size big brother. But, like the edelweiss to the Swiss, probably half its value lies not in its beauty, great though that may be, but in the danger involved in acquiring the seedling and the difficulties attendant on its development. One of the most famous Japanese habitats of the species is Mt. Ishizuchi, on Shikoku Island. Here are vast cliffs and perpendicular crags, and it is on the sides and in the clefts of these that the juniper grows. The treasure seeker must scale the precipice, or dangle spider-like on a rope from the lip of the heights above. Then, precariously, he loosens the seedling, with as much soil as he can get with it, from the face of the rock. Not always is the supporting rope equal to the weight, but worn and abraded by the sharp edge of the overhanging cliff, gives way, hurling the plant hunter into the cloud-filled valley thousands of feet below.

Under these conditions, not many of the precious seedlings reach the grower. When they do, they are planted carefully in the same type of soil from which they have been removed. But despite great pains, only a small proportion survive—twenty per cent being the generally accepted figure.

Both cost and value of the wild juniper, therefore, are high.

Fortunately, not all wild seedlings call for so hazardous a method of collection. The observant collector will often find shoots in the forest, by a stream, in the orchard, or even in his own back yard; baby trees, growing from seeds planted by nature. These may be carefully removed and placed in either seedling beds or individual pots. To insure minimum damage to the roots, as much earth as possible should be removed with them. The same type and composition of soil must be used in re-planting. Even so, the treelet suffers somewhat, and it may be anything from a couple of months to a couple of years before it has regained sufficient health to endure the handling entailed in dwarfing procedures.

As an alternative to seedlings found growing in their natural state, the grower may start his tree from a cutting. Here he has the advantage of being able to choose a small branch or twig which shows indication of growing into the shape he plans for his tree. Trite though the quotation is, the fact that "as the twig is bent the tree's inclined" is still true, especially among dwarfs. A "Y" shape, or a trunk dividing into two, or a trunk sharply inclining to left or right a little above the bole, is more easily achieved when the form is already inherent in the twig.

But here again, the mortality rate is fairly high. In fact, the cherry, peach and plum, which the Japanese dwarf tree grower frequently starts in this way, are, according to American horticultural experts, "not propagated by cuttings." The disagreement is probably the result of a basic difference in psychology. The American likes efficiency. He sees no point in wasting time on a five, ten, or twenty per cent chance. The Japanese, conversely, sees no fault in taking an infinitude of pains and much time if he can produce precisely what he wants—in fact, the pains and time add materially to the value of his achievement.

The season for cutting or slipping depends on the type of tree. (A chart covering the best types for dwarfing is appended to this chapter). The slips should be planted in a specially prepared bed, and must be carefully tended until the roots form and develop.

The composition of the soil of the cutting bed should be

**U-SHAPED
INCISION**

**BOUND
WITH MOSS**

PLATE 8: Four steps in layering.

that best suited to the particular species of tree. (Again, see chart.) The earth should be loosened and all lumps removed, by putting through a coarse sieve if necessary. Sand should be added, to insure good drainage and avoid clodding and hardening. Slips should be planted at an angle, rather than upright, and should be covered with soil to a depth of two to three inches.

If no garden space is available for a bed, pots or deep trays are quite as satisfactory. Beds or trays should be placed so as to receive as much light as possible, but, once the slips are planted, they must be protected from too much direct sunlight. A canopy of unbleached muslin, raised a foot or more above the cuttings, is very satisfactory; shades of very fine split bamboo may also be used, provided they are not so coarse as to cut off too much light. The soil must be kept moist, but not wet, so the roots may develop without rotting.

Layering is a variant of cutting or slipping, but is peculiar in that the roots are allowed to form before the twig is separated from the tree. The grower selects his twig or small branch again with an eye to the form eventually desired. Then, a couple of inches below where he plans to detach the twig, he makes a small, U-shaped incision, cutting through the cambium layer. A thick packing of peat or moss is bound around the branch over the incision, much as a surgeon will pack a wound (Plate 8). If the "dressing" is kept moist, roots begin to form, and the twig may then be detached from its parent tree and planted in its own pot.

Layering is best undertaken in spring, when the sap begins to run. In most trees, the sap rises through the inner part of the tree, returning through the cambium layer. If this layer is injured, congestion results, and when the wound is well protected by moist moss, rootlets are sent out.

The grafting method is rarely used by the conservative fancier of the traditional dwarf tree, for the graft is all too likely to result in an unsightly bulge, detracting greatly from the perfection ultimately desired. However, it is occasionally resorted to, and a well-shaped twig may be grafted onto a healthy root base.

Grafting may also be used to achieve special effects, attractive simply because they are odd. A New Year's gift of distinction in Japan is a flowering dwarf with blossoms in two, three, or (very rarely) four different shades. The gift of a

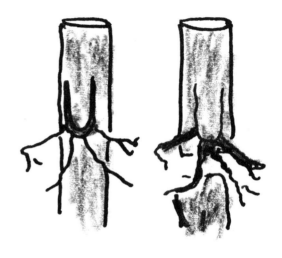

MOSS REMOVED
AFTER ROOTS
FORM

UNWANTED
LOWER END
CUT OFF

PLATE 8: Four steps in layering. (continued)

dwarf itself indicates that the recipient is regarded as a man of discrimination, appreciative of cultural values. The choice of a multi-colored dwarf suggests that he is also known for a slight originality, a liking for the unusual, even the outré, within, of course, the confines of good taste. This variegated effect is achieved by grafting. The peach is particularly well adapted to this treatment, for its flowers may be white, pink, or red, and when a branch of each shade is grafted onto one root, the result is quaint and charming in the extreme. The writer has even seen a branch of dwarf lemon grafted onto a dwarf orange.

Grafting is also sometimes used to achieve, in a hurry, those peculiar effects wherein a tree is made to look like a crane, with long legs, curving neck and outspread wings, or a sampan, its jutting prow balanced by a slender sweep and topped with a square-rigged sail—trees which, like the clipped box of Old England, may look like anything on earth except trees.

But such complicated grafting processes call for extraordinarily well developed technical skill, plus more than a little luck, and are not advised unless the grower is either an expert or can afford to be very prodigal of both trees and time.

The slowest, though in many ways the most satisfactory way of starting a dwarf tree, then, is from seed. Of course the time required depends upon the kind of tree (see chart). Seeds of the citrus fruits, for instance, can germinate in anything from a few days to a few weeks, and the little plants are relatively hardy. The cherry and plum, on the other hand, are proverbially among the slowest to develop to a satisfactory stage. The main advantage of growing the tree from seed is that since a number may be planted, one is fairly sure of having a choice of seedlings. Also, since they do not need to be moved for some time, the roots have a chance to develop healthily.

The preparation of the seed bed and treatment of the seeds is similar to the process employed with cuttings. When the seedlings are three to four inches in height, they may be transplanted into containers. Spring or fall are the best seasons for transplanting most seedlings, though the citrus does best if transplanted in winter.

The accompanying chart* shows the type of soil, germi-

* Information given is for average American climatic conditions, rather than Japanese, and was supplied through the cooperation of Dr. C.E. Dickinson, of the Lincoln University (Mo.) Department of Agriculture.

DATA ON DWARF TREES

Adjusted for average American conditions

Prepared by: Dr. C. E. Dickinson, Ph.D., Director, Horticultural Department, Lincoln University, Missouri

Tree	Type of Soil	Seed Germination Period	Slipping Season	Transplanting Season	Pruning Season
Pine	Poor, well-drained, sandy loams	30 to 60 days*	Difficult to root by cuttings**	In Japan, autumn. In U.S., spring generally preferable	Late winter before growth starts
Spruce	Almost any well-drained soil	30 to 60 days	Winter	In Japan, autumn. In U.S., spring generally preferable	Late winter before growth starts
Elm	Rich and moist	few weeks	Summer	Spring or fall	Any time, preferably late winter
Maple	Variable with different species. Silver and red maples prefer loams	few weeks	Difficult to root by cuttings**	Spring or fall	Late winter, before growth starts
Birch	Mostly in moist sandy loam or rocky subsoil. Some thrive in dry soils	60 days*	June or July	Spring or fall	Late winter

Apple	Prefer rich, well drained soil; deep. Clay loam, rich in humus, underlaid with gravel or shale is excellent	60 to 90 days*	Difficult to root by cuttings**	Spring preferable	Late winter
Cherry	Deep, gravelly or shaley loams that drain rapidly. Sour cherry is not particular as to soil type	120 days*	Not propagated by cuttings*	Spring preferable	Late winter
Peach	Adapts itself to all soils except heavy, rich ones. Sandy loams and other light soils are preferred	120 days or more*	Not propagated by cuttings**	Spring preferable	Late winter
Plum	Any well-drained garden soil a choice is available, use heavy clay loams for European varieties and lighter soils for Japanese and American varieties		Not propagated by cuttings**	Spring preferable	Late winter
Citrus	Any well-drained garden soil. Avoid extremes of clay or sand	30 days or more	Can be propagated by cuttings, but best plants not obtained this way	Winter	Just before new growth starts
		*Stratification period	**Though the tree is not normally started in this fashion, the Japanese dwarf grower does use the method, as explained in the text; but the mortality rate is high.		

nation period, and slipping and transplanting seasons for the ten most popular types of dwarf trees.

It was stated at the beginning of this chapter that Japanese *bon-sai* fanciers accept five methods of starting a tree. For those who are concerned more with results than with the exactitudes of tradition, we may add one more: Find a good nursery, and select some seedlings a few inches high. Thus one avoids the longest (and possibly dullest) period of *bon-sai* production, is fairly well assured of a healthy plant, and may start almost immediately on the most interesting phase, that of training the tree.

Diligence is the mother of good fortune.
—CERVANTES: *Don Quixote*
(Peter Anthony Motteux, trans.)

8

Transplanting

As SOON as the cutting or seedling is large enough to be handled easily, and the roots sufficiently developed to insure continued growth, the plant may be transferred from the starting bed to its individual container. From then on, for the rest of its life, the tree will have to be repotted at intervals. In the early years, of course, considerations of size and arrangement will dictate the transplanting. Later, as the tree grows, there may come a time when the roots completely fill the container, to the exclusion of earth, necessitating trimming and transplanting.

Techniques of root trimming will be discussed in a later chapter (See Chapter 10, "Technique of Trimming Branches and Roots"). In general however methods of transplanting remain the same at all stages.

The construction of the pot, and the lower drainage

layers of gravel and sand have already been described. The upper layer of soil, in which the tree actually grows, should be provided according to the preferences of the kind of tree. Some like a preponderance of leaf mould; some like loam, others prefer sand, and some will, considerately, grow in any reasonably fertile soil. The Japanese, as a working rule, use a mixture of one-half red earth and one-half loam and sand, or, preferably, leaf-mould and sand. The sand is a preventive against clodding, and the red earth helps avoid root rot immediately after re-potting. However, if the tree has been left several years without transplanting, it may need additional nourishment, and then greater proportions of loam or leaf-mould are used.

The soil must be carefully prepared for potting. First it must be thoroughly dried, which condition the Japanese achieve by spreading it on large, shallow trays in the sun. Then it is sieved, the fine particles which pass through the sieve being discarded, as they tend to clod and solidify when wet. Any sticks, stones, or heavy clods are also removed from the earth remaining in the sieve. Alternatively, one may use the prepared soil obtainable at many retail stores. It has the advantages of being uniform in quality, and sterilized.

PLATE 9: Tree with roots embracing a rock, some free-standing, some clinging in fissures. Note also use of sand as contrast and highlight.

Sand is then added and mixed well. The expert grower can become highly technical on the matter of sand. "Sharp" sands are considered preferable to "round", such as is found on the seashore or in river beds, where the constant movement and abrasion have smoothed the edges. Certain localities in Japan are noted for certain types and qualities of sand, and growers have their individual preferences. Here in America, sand is very likely to be—just sand. The important consideration is that some sand—and it must be clean—be mixed with the earth.

A thick layer of the prepared soil mixture is spread over the drainage layers in the container. It is now ready for the tree.

In transplanting, as much of the old soil as possible is removed from around the roots, which are then carefully arranged over the fresh earth in the container. If the tree is a seedling being transplanted for the first time, the trunk should be held at the angle required by the completed design, then, with the tree held firmly in place, the remaining earth is packed around the roots.

The levelling of the surface of the soil in the pots is a matter for consideration also. Some fanciers like it well banked around the bole of the tree, sloping downward toward the perimeter of the pot. Others feel that this endangers the tree, since, when it is watered, the water will naturally seek the lowest level around the edges, leaving the roots in the center almost dry. This group prefers to bank the earth around both the base of the tree and the perimeter of the pot, so that the moisture will be caught and held around the roots. There is much to be said for this latter style on aesthetic as well as technical grounds, for the slight curvature adds greatly to the beauty of the finished product.

As a further aid to appearance, a film of rich, dark earth may be spread over the surface of the soil, or moss or sand may be applied. Since these two last are suitable for use only for the well-developed tree, or one which will not be disturbed for several years, discussion of artistic theory and methods of application will be postponed until a later chapter. The dark soil, however, is easy to spread, and does increase the natural appearance of even young trees. Its chief drawback is that it has a tendency to splash muddily when the tree is watered, so either great care must be used, or the pot, when being watered, should be placed where a little mud does not matter.

The method and amount of watering is one of the most crucial considerations in the growing of dwarf trees . . . . . . probably because, though branch pruning takes place only at intervals of as much as a year, and root trimming as much as five years, watering must be attended to all the time.

It is quite as dangerous, if not more, to water too much as too little. Roots, when they are transplanted, like to rest for a few days. This is particularly true of roots which have been trimmed, for the trimming diminishes the power of absorption, and too wet a soil results tragically in rotting. Strong, healthy trees may be quite safely left outdoors in sun, breeze and rain; in fact, they rather enjoy advantages provided by Nature herself—in moderation, of course, for they like severe storms or blazing sun no better than the more sentient part of creation. But the recently transplanted tree should be carefully protected from both sun and wind, and should never be left out in the rain. After a week or two, it may, like the human convalescent or discreet sunbather, be gradually exposed.

One more word of warning: The chlorination, fluoridation, and other -ations employed by beneficent officialdom for the good of its human charges, are definitely harmful for dwarf trees. Healthy though they may be, their tiny roots and delicate leaves are certainly not adjusted to deal with the exigencies of contemporary metropolitan life. The leaves are sufficiently hard put to it to do their job in an atmosphere compounded of gasoline, coal, oil, and natural gas fumes, not to mention, in most homes, cigarette smoke. To require the roots to deal with heavy doses of man-mixed chemicals is expecting too much of them altogether.

The ideal, of course, (excluding the circumstances of recent root trimming just referred to) is the watering provided by a light, gentle shower of rain. The provident, forethoughtful grower may also catch and store rain water for use in between showers. Collecting rain water may, in the city, be something of a problem, but should not be an insurmountable one. A good storm will easily provide a couple of quarts, even a gallon or more, which will go a long way with the little trees. A drive into the country, too, will give opportunity for getting any amount of spring, stream, well, or pond water which, since they are also natural, are as good as rain.

And, if you run out of rain or natural water, distilled

(or plain home boiled and cooled) water may be used. This is not too satisfactory, for the natural minerals the trees need have been removed in the distillation process; but at least it contains nothing harmful, and the careful application of fertilizers will help fill the deficiency. While distilled water should not be used exclusively, it is a good emergency standby.

The trees should be watered carefully and gently. Since the leaves themselves like a bath, to cleanse them of dust and impurities and allow them to breathe, a sprinkling can should be used. The holes must be fairly small, however, so the deluge is not too heavy. A clothes sprinkler serves the purpose well. A spray-gun (new, of course) such as is used with liquid insecticides, is almost perfect, for there is the additional advantage that it can be directed at the tree from almost any angle, so that even the underside of the leaves can be washed,

PLATE 9a: Tree with roots embracing and growing out of a rock.

to keep them free of dust, and more importantly, insect pests and parasites.

It is important that water reaching the roots be evenly distributed. This is the reason that a sprinkler, rather than a pitcher, should be used, for the latter tends to deposit too much water is one spot and not enough in another.

Nor should the water be too cold. In fact, in the heat of summer, slightly warm water is better than chilled, especially if the leaves and foliage are to be sprinkled. And in the case of the exposed root type of dwarf, water must, in summer, be slightly warm (see Chap. 10).

In time take time while time doth last
For time is no time when time is past.
—ANON.

9

BY THE time the trees are two or three years old, or even earlier if they are of a very swift-growing species, they will be ready for the training of trunk and branches to start. Shaping is achieved by wrapping or bracing with wire, or even by applying clamps. As these training devices may have to be left in place eighteen months or more, it is very important that they be correctly applied at the outset.

This is where it becomes vitally necessary to have a clear concept of exactly how you want your branches or trunk to look. Experiment all you want to with sketches, twigs, or even pipe cleaners. But don't try it on the living tree. We have seen impulsive amateurs attack a tiny tree, bend its trunk this way and bind its branches that; decide that the appearance leaves something to be desired, remove the binding,

Training Branches and Trunks

and twist the tree in some other direction . . . . . undo it all and try yet a third effect. Then, indifferent to injured bark and damaged fibres, they wonder why the tree dies.

So even though your tree, when wired, does not look quite as you had planned, it is better to leave it alone. It may not be perfect, but at least it will be alive.

We have been speaking in terms of a single tree. However, if your plan calls for two or three or more in a unified grouping, they may all be treated at one time.

Generally, the early spring, when the sap is rising, is the best season for the application of these training devices. It should never be tried in fall or winter; though, oddly, the five-needled pine (Pinus Pentaphylla) is an exception to this rule, and thrives best when training is begun in mid-winter. This type should be transplanted not oftener than once in three years, about the end of November, and training devices are put on in January.

Traditional Japanese training materials are copper wire, hemp, and wood (this last for heavy clamps if needed.) The American modern may substitute insulated copper wire for the bare type, and friction tape or rubber, either sheet or sponge, may be used instead of the hemp, which is more difficult to obtain here.

Occasionally the wire is wound directly on the trunk or branch. However, if the tree has an exceedingly soft bark, easily injured, (as many have) or if a bend is to be made at a sharp angle, some protection is necessary, and for this the hemp, rubber or tape are used.

Hemp should be thoroughly softened in water. Several layers are placed around the branch, extending well above and below the area to be bound by wire. The first layers are fairly loose, the outer one tight, to keep the others in place. Friction tape or thin strips of rubber may be substituted for the hemp, if desired. Friction tape has the disadvantage of being sticky, and therefore hard to handle and quite difficult to remove. Both these occidental materials also have the disadvantage of looking definitely un-Oriental; the hemp, being a natural material itself, is somehow more in keeping with the dwarf tree atmosphere.

In applying the wire, the problem is to wind it tightly enough to train the tree, but not so tightly as to damage it. Remembering that it must be left in place for possibly as long as two years, it is obvious that the branch will increase in girth before the binding is removed. If the wire is wrapped too closely around the branch, the latter will swell and bulge; the flow of sap is retarded, then stops, and the tree dies. Even if this ultimate tragedy is avoided, the swelling will remain—like an old lady's knuckle bulging above her wide gold wedding band.

There is one more word of caution. Copper wire is most frequently used for binding because of its peculiar softness. However, it has another quality less desirable for dwarfing trees, namely, its terrific power to absorb heat. In summer, especially if the tree is left in the sunlight, the wire may even become too hot to touch. It may scorch the tree. Hence the suggestion that insulated wire be used. Uninsulated, or bare, wire, should be covered in summer with a thin layer of paper, to prevent overheating.

When a branch is to be trained, the wire should first be securely anchored around the trunk. The first turn of the wire should overlap the end, so as to keep it in place (Plate 10). If the wire is simply twisted in a spiral, with free ends, it is apt suddenly to unwind, flying off like a spring uncoiling, possibly injuring the tree, certainly undoing hours of painstaking work.

A branch which is to bend to the right should be wound to the left; conversely, a branch to bend to the left should be wound to the right. As the branch is bent further and further, the pressure of the wire becomes greater. Care must be taken that the branch does not snap. If the pressure seems to increase too greatly, the wire should be loosened temporarily, to be wound more tightly only when the branch begins to accustom itself to its new position.

When it comes to shaping the trunk, it must be remembered that since this is considerably thicker and therefore less malleable than the branches, more pressure must be exerted. Even greater precautionary measures are therefore necessary to prevent harm to bark and fibre. Trees with brittle wood and a tendency to snap with ease (such as persimmons, and others which turn red in autumn) must be treated with special care, and certainly no bending should be attempted when the tree is old.

If only a slight incline is required, a wire binding may be sufficient. However, if the trunk is to bend at any considerable angle (such as the tree leaning over the precipice, where the angle may be as much as 60 degrees) stronger and firmer measures are called for, and clamps may be used.

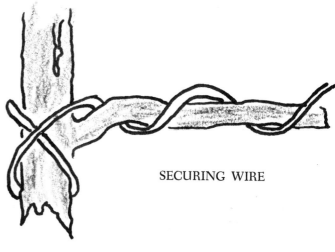

SECURING WIRE

PLATE 10: Technique of applying training wires to branches.

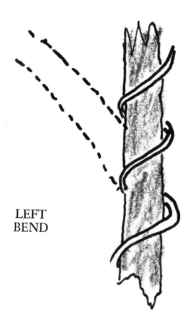

LEFT
BEND

PLATE 10: Technique of applying training wires to branches. (continued)

It is reported that the modern Japanese, as inclined to mechanical gadgets as his American counterpart, has at his disposal specially constructed screw clamps for shaping his dwarf trees. The writer admits to never having seen them, and certainly disapproves of the idea on aesthetic and ideological grounds. One thing a dwarf tree is not, is mechanical. For centuries the Japanese grower has whittled and carved his own clamps to the exact size and shape desired for his individual tree, and this the American grower can do equally well. Using a soft, easily carved wood, the grower whittles a block to the required curve or angle. If he wishes, he may use two blocks, with matched convex and concave surfaces.

Since it would probably damage the bark to bend it forcibly against the hard, unyielding wooden surface of the clamp, adequate protective packing must be used. Damp hemp is the traditional material. Materials more easily obtainable over here, and equally efficient, are sponge rubber or even strips cut from automobile inner tubes.

These padded blocks are placed against the trunk, which is bent against them and bound in place with wire. It must be remembered that the trunk itself must also be protected by some sort of packing, against being cut by the wire. Great care must be taken in binding the trunk. If too much pressure is applied, it may snap. It is better to bend it a little at a time, only gradually tightening the bindings and thus increasing the angle.

After it is bound, the trunk, like the branches, must be checked carefully at intervals to see that the bindings are not so tight as to cause cutting or swelling. If there is danger of this, they must be loosened.

It may be eighteen months to two years before the trunk will retain its shape of its own accord after the training devices are removed. They may be taken off, of course, long before this, and the tree will seem to keep its shape, but the effect will be only temporary. While the tree will probably not revert entirely to its natural shape, it will certainly depart from plan, and will grow "half bond, half free."

Such half-trained "quickies" are often palmed off on the unsuspecting in Japan, by dwarf-tree shysters—for such exist —particularly at the New Year, when the demand for miniature trees is at its height. The writer was the recipient of one such gift. Though an 18-inch high cherry in bloom, the tree

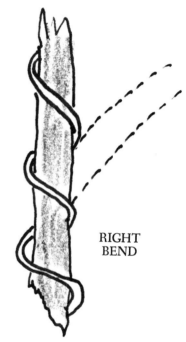

RIGHT BEND

PLATE 10: Technique of applying training wires to branches. (continued)

was exceptionally unlovely to begin with, its trunk twisted into an unwholesomely abnormal "double-S." (One suspects the basis of its selection was the theory that "foreigners" like peculiar things, and this was definitely peculiar.) In spring, the growing season, the trunk began to uncoil below, and shoot up perpendicularly above. Too ugly to be given house-room, it was planted in the back yard. Ten years later it was still there, a young tree, fair and lovely except for the lower trunk, which, for the first three or four feet, looked like nothing so much as a cross-section of an overgrown washboard.

Cut is the branch that might have grown
full straight.
—CHRISTOPHER MARLOWE: *Tamburlaine the Great*

10

Technique of Trimming Branches and Roots

THE shaping of trunk and limbs is not the only technique involved in producing a dwarf tree of desirable style. The ultimate achievement in concrete and visible form of that Ideal which the grower conceives as perfection for that individual tree, that nice balance of elements, is as much dependent upon the selection of branches as upon their sweep and curvature. And while it is not possible to manufacture a branch where none grows, elimination can be as effective as addition. For this, pruning is necessary. As a matter of fact, pruning serves the double purpose of removing unwanted twigs or branches, and of encouraging heavier, more luxuriant growth on those that remain.

In the same way, the actual dwarfing results, in measure at least, from careful root trimming. Though the confining of the roots in a small pot and the withholding of food (in the shape of soil and fertilizer) are the basic causes of dwarfing, the periodic cutting of the roots is also an element in the process. Not only does the trimming of the roots keep the tree small; the removal of long roots has the effect of forcing the development of new ones, fresh, vigorous and healthy, which keep the tree in sound condition.

Though the roots are trimmed far less frequently than the branches, it is practical to discuss the two techniques together, since tools and methods are essentially similar.

Obviously shears are the first necessity. The Japanese shears have short pointed blades, and enormous semi-circular handles which allow the user to grip with his whole fist rather than simply with thumb and forefinger, as is the case with our scissors. They are, for the unaccustomed, difficult to handle; and the American grower would be better advised to select a pair with which he can work effectively, rather than be ruled by stylistic considerations. In this case, it is the efficiency of the implement which counts, not the shape of the handles.

Probably three pairs of shears will be needed: one with long, slender blades for reaching among the branches; one with shorter blades for delicate work on leaves, twigs and rootlets; and a heavy pair for the thicker branches, trunk, or main roots. For heavy work, it is true, the Japanese sometimes uses a very fine saw. However, in inept hands a saw can do a great deal of damage, not only to the trunk or limb being worked on but on surrounding ones which may be nicked if the saw slips. A pair of good, heavy shears is far safer, and will be strong enough for all but the largest and oldest dwarfs.

Fitting the shears to the user's hand is, of course, a personal and individual matter. The quality of the blade is not. The blade must be very sharp and the two edges must fit closely, so that the cut is perfectly straight and clean. A dull pair of shears, or one whose blades do not quite meet, will tear the limb and the twigs will be broken instead of cut. We are all familiar with the appearance of a stem removed with a blunt knife or shears, ragged as if it had been chewed rather than cut off. This causes the surrounding area to dry out, the wound does not heal properly, and the whole tree may be damaged as a result. In root trimming, the injuries are less visible at the time. However, a torn or damaged root cannot absorb moisture, will get dirt-clogged and eventually rot, again causing considerable damage.

Trees are rather like humans. A wound made with a clean, sharp knife heals fairly readily; a jagged tear less quickly or easily. In the former case scarring will be minimal; in the latter the result is an ugly disfigurement. And any wound is better treated at once. Certainly, a few tiny twigs may be removed cleanly, with sharp shears, without any damage. But if a major branch is to be removed, the edges of the wound must be trimmed clean with a sharp knife and the whole area covered with some adhesive material such as sticky clay or plaster, to prevent drying out. If this is done, the cambium layer will send out new growth and within a short time the tree will have recovered from its surgery.

This careful repair work is especially necessary if through mishap, such as a slip of shears or saw, some other portion of the tree is injured. If the bark is unduly torn or the cambium layer deeply injured, the best one can hope for is a deep scar; the worst one may fear is a decayed branch. So wounds may not be treated lightly. It is better also to do repair work as one goes along. Again, trees, like humans, should not be left to "bleed."

So much for the practical method. When it comes to aesthetic considerations, not of *how* but of *where* to prune, no rules can be laid down. It is up to the grower to decide which branches to shorten; which to trim in the hope of a heavier growth; and which to remove altogether, to obtain the desired effect. Unfortunately, there is no margin for error. Once a branch is removed, it stays that way. It cannot be put back. So trimming proceeds slowly. The Japanese dwarf tree grower will sit before his tree for an hour, studying it; will bend forward and gently detatch—one leaf! Complete pruning will hence be a matter of days. The occidental, not brought up in a cultural tradition which values contemplation for its own sake, less accustomed (unless he is a chess player) to hours of deliberate gazing, will probably complete the job more quickly. But certainly constraint and consideration are advisable.

There is, of course, a difference between "heavy" pruning and "trimming," the former the removal of unwanted branches and twigs, the latter the picking off of tinier stems or leaves. Heavy pruning should be done once a year, in most cases in late winter (see chart, chapter 7), or before the new spring growth starts. Individual leaves or the smaller twigs may be removed whenever they grow in undesired places. However, in the case of flowering trees, such as cherry, peach and plum, care must be taken not to interfere with the flower buds.

Root trimming is properly undertaken only once every few years, and then when the tree is to be transplanted into fresh earth. Methods of trimming vary. Some growers, when the roots have completely filled the container, will remove the tree and, with a very sharp hatchet, simply chop off the roots all around, equi-distant from the trunk. Others will almost meticulously clean and disentangle the roots, then with a pair of very sharp shears, carefully remove all that are too long or too old. Of the two, the latter method would certainly seem the safer, as it affords less possibility of breaking or tearing.

Once the roots are trimmed, the tree should be repotted immediately in fresh earth. For a few days at least it should be watered sparingly, as the newly cut roots do not absorb moisture readily, and rot may set in.

PLATE 11: Tree drooping as if hanging over a cliff. (The vertical line in the background is a fold in the screen against which the tree was photographed.)

11

Against the dark blue sky, the autumn moon
Paints shadows of the pines.*
　　　　—Haiku by RANSETSU (1653-1707)

Exposed Root Techniques

AMONG the most appealing of dwarf trees are those which seem to be growing on, or out of, a rock, the roots above ground instead of below it, twisted, gnarled and weather-beaten. These "exposed root" trees (Plates 9, 9a) are valued highly by the Japanese, both for their beauty of form and for the philosophy of life they epitomize. They have an atmosphere all their own. Tenaciously encircling the hard rock, their roots stretch and reach for what sustenance they can. They are the symbol of all who have met the worst that life can bring, have survived, unconquered, the havoc of storm and tempest, and now rest serene with the calm tranquility of proven strength.

This type of tree is not excessively difficult to grow, but it does require time and attention.

Here again one must start with a clear picture in mind.

* Aozora ni/Matsu wo kaitari/ Kyo no tsuki.

Sometimes a boulder-shaped rock will support a single tree. Or, in imitation of the eroded slopes of the Japanese mountains and sea coast, a whole grove may rest on a vast, flat slab, the roots in a spreading tangle across the face and down the sides. The roots may hug closely the deep seams and fissures of the crag, or may curve away, as if once-protective earth had been washed away by rain and river.

Naturally, selection of both "growing rock" and tree is tremendously important. There are a few fairly standard conventions, based on entirely reasonable aesthetic considerations. For the single stone type, a tree with a tall trunk, or one particularly large in circumference, is obviously unsuitable, as the former results in poor balance, and the latter in loss of emphasis. Much better is a tree with one branch starting low down, sweeping outward to some length. (The upper branches, in this case, may be trained to whatever size, length or style that seems appropriate.) The grove effect, on the other hand, calls for trees with straight, comparatively slender trunks, the first branch growing some distance from the ground. Thick trunks and low branches cause too crowded an effect.

In arranging the trees on the rock, the Japanese artistic

sense, in consonance with Nature's, demands an off-center effect. Never should the base of the trunk be squarely centered on the rock, with roots spread evenly down on all sides. Rather, one or two main roots stretch in the same direction, almost, but not quite, parallelling the main branch, and the rest cling wherever the security of the tree requires. Even with the slab and grove effect, the trees will be grouped along one edge, the roots stretching across the broad, flat face of the rock. But on no account should the roots stretch one way and the branches another. That would be most unnatural.

Since very long roots are necessary for this arrangement, the tree so destined should be left in its pot for five or six years, until its roots, undisturbed and untrimmed, have grown to considerable length. These years may be employed in training the trunk and branches. The tree is then removed, the roots carefully straightened, and arranged over the rock. (An alternative method of producing long roots reasonably quickly is described at the end of this chapter.)

The relation between the size of the rock and the length of the roots is important. A fair proportion of the roots must be stretched over and around the rock so as to meet beneath it. If they are too short, they do not grip the rock sufficiently, and the tree may overbalance. If, on the other hand, the rock is too small, the whole effect will be lost, for in the beginning especially, the base must be covered with soil to the depth of an inch or so if the roots are to obtain nourishment. For the slab and grove effect, the surface area must be large enough to allow arrangement without crowding. The beginner, with no experience to guide, will probably be well advised to provide himself with several rocks of differing sizes; for if the rock he has chosen is too large or too small, he cannot very well leave the tree uprooted while he goes to look for another one!

The arrangement of the roots over the rock is one thing which cannot be too exactly planned in advance, for it will depend on the number and length of the roots; and since the little roots are rather delicate, too much experimentation is unsafe. Generally, however, some satisfactory effect can be arrived at. The roots do not need to hug the rock too closely. In fact, if they seem inclined to curve or spring away from the rock in places, so much the better. It will give the coveted effect of eroded cliffs. If there are seams or fissures, probably one or two of the roots can be made to lie along these.

The larger proportion of the roots must be carried over

PLATE 11a: Tree bending sharply, as if drooping over a cliff.

and underneath the rock, those from either side meeting beneath it, holding the tree secure.

Then comes the job of keeping the roots where you want them. The Japanese use a cord made of palm fiber, but any garden cord will do as well, provided it is not too thin (which would cut the rootlets) and is of a material which will eventually rot in the earth, to make removal simpler when the time for removal comes. Unfortunately, it is extremely easy to damage the delicate roots in this tieing-on process. If the outer bark is broken, serious injury may result.

Once tied in place, roots and stone are plastered over completely with a protective covering of mixed clay and peat, then potted, with the lower surface of the stone sunk well in the soil, which should at this stage be brought up at the sides also. Not until later, when the roots have had a chance to become well established, need the base of the rock alone be soil-embedded.

In the early stages, the grower must guard against damage to the roots through drying out or burning. The packing must be kept fairly moist; but since it is malleable, and the roots, trying to follow their own devices, have a way of poking through the covering, a few extra daubs of clay may have to be applied every week or so for the first year. Actually, making the clay adhere is no easy job; it quite persistently falls off. By the end of the year, however, the roots will have become more compliant. The packing may then be removed, and any unsightly or unnecessary rootlets carefully trimmed off. Once more the clay-peat packing is applied and the tree re-planted. This time, though the base of the rock should be sunk fairly deep, the soil need not be brought so far up the sides. The roots, stronger now, need less protection, but as the packing gradually washes off in the watering, exposing them by degrees, they will provide themselves with a hard, protective bark, like that of the trunk itself.

This tieing, packing, daubing and re-daubing, unpacking and re-packing is at best a tricky process. There is an easier, and somewhat safer, method which may be recommended for beginners. The processes, up through the tieing of the roots in place, are the same. The rock-bound root may then be packed in a small burlap sack, filled with the type of soil recommended for the tree, and the whole sunk in the garden. (The sack is not essential, but although it eventually rots in the garden mold, it does somewhat simplify removal from the earth.) The soil should be packed well up the trunk for an inch or so, to insure safety of the roots.

Then, after a year, the tree, root-wrapped rock and all, is removed from the soil, unnecessary rootlets trimmed off, the whole covered with the clay-peat mixture, and potted as desired. From this point on, the process is the same as that after the second packing already described.

Exposed root trees need somewhat more careful attention, especially in watering, than their well-covered brethren. In summer, particularly in the hotter parts of the country, the stones absorb heat, drying out the roots. The trees should be sprinkled carefully, on all four sides, to insure that the stone does not divert the water from some parts of the roots; also, to avoid a too great change of temperature, lukewarm, not cold, water should be used if the rocks are warm.

Exposed root trees do not need transplanting as frequently as the other types. The roots do not grow to fill the pots so swiftly, so repotting once in six to ten years is usually sufficient. More frequent moving seems to upset them, and they protest with the only means at their command—by losing some of their strength and beauty.

THE LONG-ROOTED PINE

There is one style of exposed-root dwarf which is in a class of its own, and that is the Long-Rooted Pine (Plate 5). The trunk, generally only a few inches long, but large around, is supported on a tall brace, or crutch. From one end springs a group of twisted branches tipped by tufts of needles; from the other trail roots stretching hungrily tentacle-like to the soil below. It reminds one, somehow, of the fowls of Shikoku, (Plate 13) whose tail feathers, growing 15 feet or more, necessitate their living constantly on a high perch, allowed on the ground only when a "train bearer" is along to support that fabulous tail. The birds, fanciful and unnatural though they are, are also beautiful. In the case of the pine, the beauty may, or may not, be in the eye of the beholder. Few occidentals, except the initiate, admire them, their adjectives ranging from "odd" to "ugly." To the nature-loving Japanese, they are a sort of sublimation of nature. They are indeed nature imposed

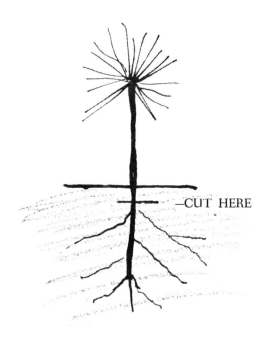

CUT HERE

PLATE 12: Steps in growing long-rooted pine.

upon by art; and there is a weird fascination in their other-worldly atmosphere.

They are also difficult to grow. And though the actual production time is, by tree dwarfing standards, not overly long, and the techniques not basically difficult, none but the genuine lover of the strange should attempt one.

Only two types of tree, the Red Pine (Pinus densiflora) and Black Pine (Pinus Thunbergii) are suitable for this treatment, and the trees must be started from seed. When the seedling is about a year old, it will be a twig, perhaps three inches in height, with a brush of pine needles at the tip. When the tuft of needles is well opened, the entire center should be pinched out, leaving only a few sets. At the same time, the root is cut off just where the tap joins the main stem (Plate 12).

The resultant twig, to all appearances an ordinary cutting, is then planted in an ordinary seedbed, and tended just like a cutting. Since, again, the rate of mortality is apt to be high, not only at this juncture but as each step progresses, it is well to start with plenty of seedlings.

During the next year, if tended and fertilized properly,

the seedlings will produce a number of rootlets, fairly well distributed on all sides, most of them of approximately the same length. Then in spring, the plants are removed from the soil, and unwanted roots cut off.

Here, the grower uses his discretion as to how many roots he wants to leave remaining, and the placement and direction of their growth. Those that do not fit into his picture are cut off; so also are all little lateral roots and feeders, except at the very tip. The remaining roots are drawn out straight, and the "trunk" of the seedling bound to a support.

It is now ready for potting. However, only the very tips of the roots are covered with soil. Again the little tree is allowed to grow for a year, then once more it is uprooted, all newly developed feeders and lateral roots removed, a longer stake provided, and the tree replanted with only the root tips below the soil.

And so, year by year, the roots stretch and strain after nourishment; and year by year the grower increases the height of the supporting crutch. He will probably, after the roots have attained a length of two feet or more, want to arrange the trunk horizontally, and may also apply light training wires

NEW ROOTS

PLATE 12: Steps in growing long-rooted pine. (continued)

Exposed Root Techniques · 89 ·

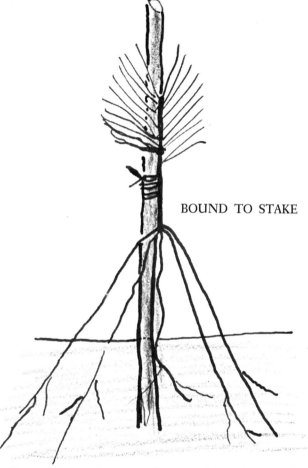

BOUND TO STAKE

to the branches, to achieve the twisted effect in consonance with the twisted roots. Some roots will grow faster than others, so while the tree is young it may be necessary to prop each root on a separate support to prevent its sagging. As the growth hardens, these auxiliary props may be removed, and the roots will retain their shape.

Given this treatment, the roots grow surprisingly fast, in the early stages sometimes as much as a foot a year.

This method of "stretching" the roots is occasionally used by the Japanese grower to produce ones long enough for use with a particularly large stone (for it would in no way distress the Japanese owner of an especially fine stone if he had to keep it some time before using it.)

And, as in the case of the tree grown on a rock, there is an alternative, and somewhat simpler, method of production. For this, a long tube with an inside diameter of about an inch, is required. The Japanese, close to nature, uses bamboo, hollowed through the center, but any material may be used, provided it can be split lengthwise. This split tube is filled with a mixture of sand and soil, the pine seedling planted in one end, and the two halves of the tube bound together. The tube is then planted vertically in the soil, either garden or pot.

PLATE 12: Steps in growing long-rooted pine. (continued)

The roots, thus planted, stretch rapidly downwards, seeking more moisture and better nourishment than is provided by the thin fare in the tube. When they finally reach the soil, the tube is unbound, the plant carefully freed, and the roots cleaned of any sand or soil which may cling to them. They are then ready to arrange in any desired fashion.

This method of long root production has one distinct advantage. The roots, well protected, are less likely to dry out than when only the tips are in the earth. It is also easier to keep the tube in an upright position, and the tiny trunk is not subject to possible damage through being bound to a support. On the other hand, there is a limit to the length of tube which may be used, and thus to the length of root which may be produced. Also, the roots, freed suddenly from protective covering, are apt to be more delicate than those which have been hardened as they grow.

In practice, the Japanese dwarf tree grower uses this long-root method mainly when he wants to produce roots quickly for the "tree on rock" technique; for with that, the tender roots are soon re-covered with peat-moss and clay, and have time to harden.

12

Caring for the Trees

Take your necessary precaution against your enemies.
—The *Koran* (Trans. by George Sale)

1. *FERTILIZERS*

ONE of the basic principles underlying the production of dwarf trees is that the withholding of food will cause stunting. Hence the tiny pots, the bare minimum of earth, the trimmed roots. Despite the enforced semi-starvation, however, some fertilization is necessary if leaves or flowers are to develop their full beauty, and plants remain healthy.

The Japanese, with their deep faith in nature and their traditional suspicion of mass production mechanics, lean heavily on natural fertilizers. Only the most modern will experiment with the chemicals on the market. (For that matter, it is only within recent years that we have been able to do so in America.) The dwarf tree grower, therefore, character-istically prefers to make, rather than buy, his fertilizers.

Among typical recipes for home-made fertilizers is the fol-lowing: Soak one-third pint soya bean cake in one-half gallon of water, until the water barely changes color. Strain out the bean-cake, and water the dwarf tree twice a week with the liquid. Another recipe calls for three medium-sized cuttle fish boiled for thirty minutes in half a gallon of water. Remove the cuttle fish, cool the liquid, and use as fertilizer. Silk worm manure may be used, but, since it is very strong, it must be soaked in water, the resultant liquid diluted until it is only faintly yellow, then used sparingly.

If, on the other hand, solid fertilizer is preferred, then dried herring or sardine are recommended. The fish should be quartered, and one piece buried in each corner of the dwarf tree container. As the tree is watered, the moisture carries the richness of the decaying fish to the roots. One advantage of this method, it is explained, is that as the fish decomposes, the soil under which it was buried falls in, so it is easy to see when more fertilizer is needed.

But, esoteric (not to say exotic) as soya bean cake, cuttle

fish, dried sardine, and even silk-worm may sound, and unprocurable as they almost surely are, the American grower need not give up hope and doom his little trees to starvation rations. There are fertilizers on the market which may be used with equal success.

It will be noted that the fertilizers preferred by the Japanese are organic (of animal origin), rather than inorganic (of mineral origin). Organic fertilizers are used to some extent in the United States, chief among them being dried blood, animal tankage, meat meal, cotton seed meal, castor bean meal, green and barnyard manure, and sheep manure. These are, however, not too easily available, especially in the small quantities which would be needed for dwarf trees. And, while it would be possible to work out, scientifically, derivatives equivalent to the Japanese fertilizers mentioned earlier,* it would, from a practical standpoint, be scarcely advisable.

Fertilizers on the American market are mainly of the inorganic type, the chief elements being nitrogen, phosphorus, and potassium. Several appearing under copyrighted trade

* Information on fertilizers supplied by Dr. J. N. Freeman, head of the Department of Agriculture of Lincoln University, Mo.

PLATE 13: The long-tailed fowl of Skikoku Island. These fowl (roosters) produced by centuries of selective breeding, grow tail feathers of extraordinary length. Tail of this specimen is ten feet, some have been reported with tails of eighteen feet. The birds, kept in specially constructed cages, are exercised by a "train bearer" who carries the tail coiled over his arm.

names may be found in any store catering to gardeners; even department and dime stores have them. Any of the standard brands sold for general use would be suitable for dwarf trees. However, those in liquid form are safer to use, for the powders are extremely concentrated, and if not completely dissolved might burn the roots of the dwarf, since they are so scantily protected by earth. Even the liquid forms should be used in considerably weaker solution than the directions call for, for the same reason.

Early spring, when the plants are just beginning to put out new leaves and shoots, is, in general, the best time for fertilizing. Fertilizer may also be applied from early to middle summer; but there should be a period of rest allowed, when the new spring growth is hardening.

2. INSECTICIDES

Probably the pests to which plants are heir, such as aphis, caterpillars, ants, and others, will not be too great a problem with the well cared for dwarf, though even these must be watched. In Japan, the dreaded enemy of the needle-bearing trees such as pines and junipers, is the "Komushi," or "dust insect," a minute organism which looks like nothing so much as grains of brownish red dust, but which can kill the tree by sucking out the moisture. The best protection against these pests is held to be a careful spraying with water twice a day, with particular attention to the underside of the leaves, where they usually hide. Fortunately, in summer, when the danger of infestation is at its height, the dwarfs like a fair amount of moisture. Even in Japan, where the climate is, on the average, considerably more humid than in most parts of America, watering twice a day is not too much. If, however, you feel that the roots may be getting too much moisture, the top of the container may be protected with a sheet of wax paper while the leaves are being sprayed. (General instructions for watering were given in Chapter 8).

Insecticides are not recommended, and, if used, must be heavily diluted.

3. CARE IN WINTER

While the dwarf trees must, of course, be protected from the extremes of heat and cold, moisture and dryness, they are unexpectedly hardy. It would be almost certainly fatal to subject them to a thorough freezing in winter; yet some cold is good for them. In fact, if they are to be placed in a hothouse for forcing, their blooms are likely to be irregular unless they have first been exposed to one or two frosts. The transition to forcing house must then be made slowly. A brief stay in the cool dark of an unheated basement or the coldroom of a greenhouse is advised, to stimulate a winter growth of root. The Japanese, who do not have either basements or cellars, but do raise their homes two or three feet above the ground on pillars, frequently keep their dwarf trees under the porch during this hardening period. They may then, little by little, be exposed to the light and sun.

Winter protection may be accomplished in various ways. In reasonably mild climates, a shelf along a sunny wall, protected at night by hanging mat screens or awnings, will be sufficient. But the Japanese, who likes to make of his trees a decoration, and is, moreover, blessed with a system of architecture which calls for full-length sliding doors instead of built-in windows, will often build a small greenhouse at one end of his porch. This permits the plants to be admired during the day; and at night, simply by opening the sliding glass doors between porch and house, the trees may be kept warm. If the air is dry, a pan of water will add moisture.

A fairly typical "semi-detached" greenhouse is shown in Plate 14. This also illustrates a popular heating device, consisting of an electric light, with a globe of low wattage, suspended over a bowl of water. The electric bulb is provided with a "petticoat" of gauze, the lower end of which touches the water, thus affording both warmth and moisture—and the danger of fire! In America, only the inveterate handyman needs to build his own greenhouse, for excellent "prefabs" are on the market, many of them designed to fit into a window.

It must be remembered, of course, that Japan as a whole enjoys a relatively temperate climate. Except in the extreme north of the main island, and in Hokkaido, zero temperatures are practically unknown. Even in winter, over most of the island, the days are sunny and mild. Hence the Japanese greenhouses, even where they exist, are much less elaborate than ours. The sun warms the glass house by day; and a covering with straw or bamboo mat-blinds retains sufficient heat at night. In many parts of America extra heat will be needed even during the daytime in winter. The warmth of a glassed-in sunporch should be adequate; and one might even suggest a sunny living room window, except that the average American living room is frequently too warm, and, blessed with central heating, almost certainly too dry, for the average dwarf tree. If it is to be kept in such a spot, it might be placed in a large, shallow pan of water; however, the water should not touch the base of the plant pot, or the roots will get too damp.

Moon and plum blossom—and lo!
The spring scene is complete.*
    —Haiku by BASHO (1649-1669)

13

POSSIBLY the most reward-
ing of trees for the dwarf enthusiast are the pine, the maple,
the cherry and the plum. The pine, in addition to being
relatively easy to train, a tree, moreover, which soon takes on
the look of age, is a "standby," for as an evergreen it never
seems to have an "off" season. The maple too is fairly tractable,
though its chief beauty lies in its foliage. This is familiar to
most of us. Yet, compared to the Japanese, the leaves of the
American maple are as burlap to gossamer. And when these
are reduced to miniature, the result is a faery thing, as gnarled
roots and dark trunk support a heavy cloud of delicate jade
in spring, dark green in summer, and glittering gold, blazing
scarlet or glowing crimson in fall.

    As for the cherry—most of us, when thinking of Japan in

* Haru mo haya/Keshiki totonou/Tsuki to ume.

The Well-Beloved Plum

terms of flowers, think of it as "the land of cherry blossoms." Probably the Japanese himself, if he were asked to name the most loved flower, would reply "the cherry blossom." It is the flower of knighthood, of chivalry, for the blossom, like the knight, does not outlive its glory. It does not wither and die, nor even "just fade away"; but the petals are shed, and they are no more. (On the other hand, the red camellia, which drops its whole flower intact, is rather disliked, despite its beauty, for the scattered flowers look, the Japanese say, like bleeding, decapitated heads lying on the pathway.)

Yet, all in all, apart from that one extremely brief period in spring, when the tree seems about to float away on a cloud of delicately scented, ethereal pink, the cherry rather lacks interest.

And the jewel of trees, in Japanese eyes, seems to be the plum, especially the dwarf plum. In fact, were one to make a statistical study, it would probably be found that the plum appears far more frequently than the cherry in poetry, art, literature and proverb. For one thing, it is a member of the main trilogy of felicitous omens: the evergreen pine because it never fades, the tough bamboo which bends but cannot be broken, and the courageous plum that puts forth its blossoms amidst the snow.

Incidentally, these "felicitous" symbols of the Japanese are worth a study in themselves. The writer owns a wall hanging on which the five standard "fortune" symbols are hand-printed on russet silk. There is the pine which, in addition to its evergeen quality, symbol of long life, is also symbolic of increasing fortune, for its needles radiate outwards from a single point—a concept, by the way, which makes the folding fan also a good luck symbol, for, like our horn of plenty, it grows ever wider. Then there is the sea turtle, emblem of long life, so old that he has grown a "tail" of seaweed; there are the plum and bamboo, for aggressive courage and fortitude; and finally the kingly crane, representing not only long life but good fortune, for his wide-spread wings are again fan-shaped. Another wall hanging pictures a carp leaping up a waterfall, typifying, of course, the "never say die" attitude. And yet a third shows Mt. Fuji, revered not only for its unearthly beauty, clearcut against the sky in lonely majesty, but because it, too, is fan-shaped.

But to return to the subject of the plum tree. Considering the fact that there are said to be some 1,500 varieties of this tree in the United States, it is not surprising that Japan claims a conservative 500; and ancient Japanese literature, according to classical scholars, mentions many, many more, such as the lavender plum, the pale yellow and deep yellow plums, the "black" plum (a very deep lavender) and a six-petalled snow white plum which are no longer in existence.*

So beloved are the dwarf plums that particularly beautiful specimens are given fanciful names. "Dragon Gate," "Sunrise on the Sea," "Flower of the Snowy Moon," "Cascading Stars" —these are only a few on record. In the case of the various species also, while some may be known by descriptive terms such as Green Calyx Plum, Winter Plum, First of August Plum, there are also the Green Dragon Plum, Plum of the Melting but Lingering Snow, and Plum of the Waning Moon in the Morning Sky. One truly extraordinary variety, The Plum of the Sleeping Dragon, originating, legend says, from the great plum of the Kameido Shrine in Tokyo, sends down long trailing branches which root banyan-like, to grow and flower in their turn.**

* Samuel Newsom, *Japan News Week,* Tokyo, Japan, March 22, 1941.
** *Ibid.*

Many of these varieties are believed to have been developed over the centuries from the *yabai* (Prunus mume), the field plum or wild plum. And while some have passed out of existence, many varieties of the *yabai* still remain, including one, the "Kaga haku" with so interesting a bark that its marking, stylized and conventionalized, forms the crest of the noble House of Kaga. The ordinary *yabai* bears five-petalled white flowers, grows almost universally in Japan, and (of prime importance to the dwarf grower) is remarkably hardy, with a fine catholicity of taste in soil and climate.

The plum, in contrast with the cherry which mantles itself in a diaphanous cloud of pink, sends out a cascade of long branches on which the flowers cling like tiny butterflies of white, pink, lavender, lilac, yellow and cerise (Plate 15).

None of these plants, it might be noted, were, or are, grown for fruit. It is a peculiar quirk of the Japanese character that, forced though they have always been to make full use of every square inch of arable ground, they are yet quite capable of asking nothing of their trees save that they be lovely to look at. Multitudinous as the cherry trees are, the edible fruit was unknown until, within modern times, fruit-bearing stock was imported from the west. The native Japanese cherry

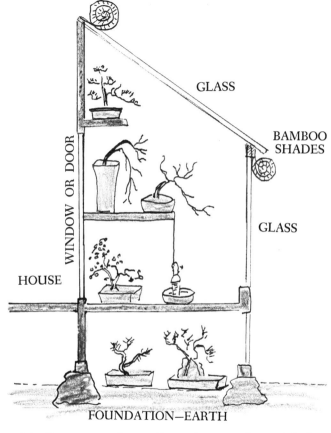

GLASS

BAMBOO SHADES

WINDOW OR DOOR

GLASS

HOUSE

FOUNDATION—EARTH

PLATE 14: Cross-section of a small greenhouse such as might be attached to the window or porch of a Japanese house. Note the makeshift heater-humidifier—an electric light bulb wrapped in a piece of cotton cloth, one end of which is immersed in water.

is a minute object consisting entirely of skin and stone, bitter and unpalatable. The plum fared somewhat better. It at least had more meat and could be salted or pickled. These pickled plums (*ume-boshi*) are an essential part of the standard Japanese breakfast, both because of their medicinal value and because their slight astringent property gives a clean, fresh feeling to the mouth. And in pre-war days, the Japanese school child's "patriotic lunch" was a flat box of boiled rice with a pickled plum in the center, representing, of course, the Japanese flag. (In winter these lunch boxes were put near the school room stove to take the chill off the rice. The devoted patriot, however, despised this sybaritic self-indulgence and laid up spiritual treasure for himself by eating his rice cold. What particular good it did would be hard to say; but the efficacy of symbolism is not necessarily to be equated with its intellectual content.)

Dwarf plum trees vary almost as much in size as they do in styling. Some of the very ancient specimens are really giants of their kind, with trunks a foot in diameter and six to eight feet tall, yet with roots that could be contained in a two-quart pot. There are also jewel-like miniatures, from a few inches to a foot high, in pots which can—and often were, by older fanciers—carried in the hand like a bouquet. It is probably a matter of individual taste, but the writer prefers the latter. Certainly they are much more practical. They are easier to handle, take up less room, and attain an appearance of age in infinitely less time!

A Japanese proverb specifies "eighteen years for a plum to bloom" if grown from seed. Fortunately, there is a quicker way of doing it. Made from a healthy cutting, a "tree" may bloom in three years, and by the time it is six years old will have all the appearance of a mature adult.

This method starts not with a seed, but with a cutting from a good healthy tree. Only cuttings from the field plum can be used; most other varieties are practically impossible to root. Cuttings should be made from last year's wood, when the trees have all but finished blooming and the leaves are starting to bud. If well-shaped twigs are chosen, ones which have inherent possibilities for training into desirable shapes, the grower's task will be easier. However, since only about one cutting in ten will survive, there may not be too much choice. Besides, what starts as a straight cutting may be trained according to the preference of the grower.

The cuttings should be made from seven to nine inches

long, certainly not less than seven. With scissors or a sharp knife, make a cross-wise cut in the lower end, being sure that the edges are clean. Torn or damaged cuttings will simply decay without rooting. Plum cuttings do best in a cold frame, in the ground, in a well-drained spot that receives plenty of sunshine. The earth should be dug and well broken up to a depth of about 18 inches, and the upper layer mixed with sand to assist drainage. In planting, the cuttings should be covered to a depth of five to six inches. Some may start producing roots in as little as four to six months, and may be carefully potted. It is best, if possible, to leave them in the cold bed until the following spring, though the climate in some sections may make this simply the greater of two risks.

Or alternatively, there is nothing in the world to prevent the dwarf tree grower from by-passing all this long process, the results of which are at best unpredictable, buy a very tiny seedling plum from the nursery, and go on from there!

Training and shaping devices may be applied when the plants are large enough, whether they are in the ground or in pots.

Potting and/or transplanting should be done when the

blossoming season is over, generally in March, but should not be attempted between April and August. The initial techniques already described in chapter eight should be used in preparing the container. For the plum, a layer of coarse red earth, with particles the size of peas, should be spread over the lowest layer of gravel in the pot, to allow good drainage. Growing soil should be prepared by mixing seven parts of good fertile earth with three parts of red (non-fertile) earth, and adding enough sand to insure that the mixture is porous.

Plums seem to like plenty of fertilizer, which may be applied twice a week from late spring to early December. If this treatment is continued, by the end of the third year the tiny trunk and limbs will have gradually thickened and assumed a look of "grown-up" maturity, and by the time it is six, the tree will begin to have that coveted look of extreme old age.

Since the branches may grow fairly rapidly on their diet of fertilizer, the grower will want to keep them trimmed and trained to the desired shape. Complete pruning is best not attempted until late autumn. After pruning, the tree should be kept in the shade for a few days, then gradually exposed to the sunlight until, in a couple of weeks, it may be left in the sun for a good part of each day. Except for the brief period immediately after root trimming and transplanting, the soil should be kept fairly moist, whether the tree is grown in the ground or in a pot. In the height of summer especially the roots tend to dry out, and plenty of water must be given.

Art is limitation; the essence of
every picture is the frame.
—G.K. CHESTERTON: *Orthodoxy*

14

THE dedicated grower regards his dwarf tree, even in its preliminary stages, as young parents regard their firstborn, unique and wholly beautiful. To the dispassionate observer its charm in these early days is that of someone else's offspring, at worst questionable, at best only incipient. But there does come a time when the tree, developed and trained, may be displayed and admired with unfeigned delight. The dwarf is gem-like, and, gem-like, its setting must be chosen with due consideration to size, color and shape. All sorts of elements enter into the correct display of the dwarf tree, from background to stand to accessory ornaments. To the many questions which arise there will, in most cases, be no single answer, and individual growers will have individual opinions regarding the same tree. Much is subjective. But there are some generalizations which may guide.

Displaying to Advantage

One decision to be made when the tree goes on display is whether the soil surface should be left uncovered. There is certainly no fault to be found with the appearance of dark, rich soil; but if covering is wanted, there is the choice of moss or white sand.

With moss, one can hardly go wrong. Nothing more quickly produces an atmosphere of age, its deep green looks cool, and its very presence suggests the untroubled rest and peace of forest glade or old orchard. Blossom-laden branches glow and gleam above its quiet depths, and the dark of evergreens is enhanced. However moss must not be allowed to grow too luxuriant or it may harm the tree. It has a tendency to absorb the fertilizer, leaving the roots hungry. Also, it holds the moisture when the tree is watered, keeping the earth below it damp and cool, both conditions which hinder the healthy growth of root. So, beautiful though the thick carpet may appear, the grower must steel his heart and at intervals thin it drastically. A few tufts left where they contribute most to the effect will soon spread the carpet again.

When background contrast is desirable, white sand is the answer. It makes a good base for the deep green of pine, juniper or spruce. It is charming below limbs heavy with cherry blossom, and striking with a maple tree, whether pale green in spring or richly colorful in fall. With plum and peach it is sometimes less satisfactory, for the ethereal delicacy of blossom may be lost above the white; here moss looks better. Sand is particularly interesting to use, for it may vary from the fineness of salt to the coarseness of gravel, from river sand to crushed white onyx, and each gives a different effect. Japanese will pay considerable sums for the fine white sand found only in certain areas; marble crushed to various degrees of fineness is more easily available, and much used. Extremely fine "round" sand has a rather flat appearance, "rough" sand and the finer grades of crushed marble, white onyx or quartz sparkle and glisten from innumerable angles and facets with a gently scintillating life.

Sand looks best with a colored container. The grower should think twice before using white sand with a white container, since this could make the base disproportionately heavy for the tree.

Since the dwarf tree is so small, scarcely larger, often, than a vase of flowers, special consideration must be given to

PLATE 15: Plum tree in blossom. Twisted trunk.

Displaying to Advantage · 113 ·

the matter of locating it to best advantage. The strictest canon of Japanese tradition prescribes that it be placed in the *tokonoma,* an integral part of every formal or public room in a Japanese home. (The word *tokonoma,* generally translated "alcove," is actually untranslatable; the literal interpretation of "bed place" is an impossible substitute; though "alcove dais" approximates the sense. Fixed at one-half *tatami* in size in a four-*tatami* tea ceremony room, in others proportioned to the room itself, the floor is raised a few inches above the rest of the room (Plate 1) and is bordered with wood, plain, but as fine in quality as the purse of the owner permits. The guest of honor is always seated in front of the *tokonoma,* but to sit on it, or set foot on it, would be a solecism of immeasurable magnitude.)

The very structure of the occidental home makes such formal display impossible, of course, for it has nothing approximating a *tokonoma;* even if it did, one can hardly imagine a guest standing—let alone kneeling—silent before it for long minutes of ritualistic admiration. This leaves the placing of the tree strictly at the discretion of the owner. To be sure, the current passion for domestic layouts featuring "areas" with "dividers" rather than homes with rooms and walls may complicate the problem, for the little dwarf shows up best against a background, is lost in the wide open spaces. But a stand in a corner, the top of a buffet, even a wall bracket—these make good display centers. Care must be taken, however, not to place the tree against a patterned wall paper, for the design will smother the tree. But some sort of background, such as a miniature screen, a great paper fan, even a hanging panel of fine grass matting, split bamboo or heavy silk will do the trick, and be entirely in keeping with the atmosphere of the tree itself.

As a matter of fact, the Japanese themselves feel perfectly at liberty to display their trees informally elsewhere than in the *tokonoma*. A collection may be arranged on a tier of shelves, even left in a semi-detached greenhouse such as is described earlier; the top of a bookcase or chest below a window may be used. Probably the cardinal tenet for such display is that the surroundings be free of distracting clutter. The writer recalls visiting a very ancient and aristocratic lady in pre-war Tokyo, the entrance hall of whose home, large and floored with wood rubbed to a high gloss by generations of servant girls, was completely empty of furniture save for a flat screen of dull gold bordered in black lacquer. Before it, in breath-taking perfection, was a dark spruce, about three feet high and doubtless as many centuries old.

In addition to the background, the stand on which the dwarf tree is set is also a matter for thought. Little but the size and shape of the tree and container, and the location, governs the choice here. If a tree angled sharply downwards is planted in a shallow container, the stand must necessarily be tall, with a surface scarcely, if at all, larger than the base of the container. On the other hand, if such a tree is in a tall, vase-like container, a low stand will be sufficient; in fact, a tall stand might throw the whole thing out of balance, making it too high for its comparative width. A tree whose height is a feature, such as the long-rooted pine, needs only a low stand, if any at all. A small tree, a mere twelve to eighteen inches tall, will require a stand at least high enough to let it be seen easily.

If the tree is to grace a buffet or table, there still remains the question of whether it should have a base. This is a matter of individual preference; but often the owner of some precious *objet d'art,* which the dwarf tree essentially is, will set it on a special base or pedestal, to highlight its individuality and distinguish it from the general mill run of ornamentation. For a real dwarf, a tiny stand two to four inches in height is excellent; or, if that is that too much, a mat of woven grasses or split bamboo serves the purpose beautifully.

Whatever its size, height or shape, the stand or base must be appropriate to the tree, natural and simple in line as possible. No brass-and-plate-glass scaffolding, certainly no iron-bar trigonometric nightmare, above all no froth of sugar-encrusted lace doilies. Wood (or stone) is the only material. It may be dark or light, plain, inlaid, or lightly carved, so long as it becomes an accessory to the tree and does not distract attention from it. Its planes and angles should be soft, gracious, unobtrusive (and like the productions of the best couturiers, the cost of such things is often in direct ratio to their simplicity.) Much prized by Japanese collectors is the type of base made from a flat wood slab, cut across the trunk of a tree, the bark still on, finished with a clear lacquer or rubbed to a high polish. Sometimes tiny one- or two-inch legs are attached, sometimes the flat slab itself is used. The natural markings of the wood, the irregularity of outline and the interest of the bark, made each example unique and characterful. Driftwood, so popular in the United States, would be singularly adaptable to use as stands for dwarf trees.

A dwarf tree is rarely shown alone, but the accompanying accessories must be selected with discrimination. In the formal setting of the *tokonoma,* a hanging scroll (*kake-mono*) is a must, plus one other ornament. Occasionally a flower arrangement is shown in combination with a dwarf tree. The writer, while hesitating to cavil at the Japanese sense of the artistic, feels this effect less than happy; for the juxtaposition of the natural-size flower and the dwarf tree, so different in scale, can make for painful distortion. Most acceptable ornament in Japanese convention is an antique incense burner, of porcelain, pottery or bronze; or a stone, water-stone or sand-and-stone arrangement suggestive of some natural scene or aspect (of which more in a subsequent chapter.) The American grower, free from the singular exigencies of an extremely complex artistic tradition, which both proscribes and prescribes according to mysterious historic, mythological, literary, philosophical and artistic allusions of which the ordinary Japanese himself is often ignorant, can please himself when it comes to auxiliary ornament. With the full sweep of orient and occident from which to draw, he may make up his own settings: a fishing boat with the pines of Monterey; a log cabin under a flowering apple tree; a tiny anvil under a dwarf chestnut, or a miniature Stonehenge beside a druidical oak—these last having a nice literary flavor of which even the Japanese would approve.

Or he may simply enjoy his little tree for its own immaculate delicacy!

15

Amidst insects' drone, the hamlet
Lies closed in sleep.*
　　　　　　　—Haiku by GETTO

Miniature Landscapes—
A Sister Art

DURING those quiescent seasons, those long periods when the dwarf trees seem to require little but fresh air, light and water, the grower may find it interesting to extend his hobby from miniature trees to miniature landscapes in general, recognized as a sort of sister art by the Japanese themselves.

Rocky, storm-lashed sea coasts, the quiet grandeur of hills, torrents dashing down precipitous crags, limpid lakes and slow-flowing rivers, peaceful hamlets and tree-shadowed temples—all these are produced in miniature with rocks, sand, tiny plants and lifelike figurines set out upon a tray. Some arrangements are strictly classical in both style and material, intended to arouse the intellectual imagination of the informed; others are frankly "popular," in fact rather frowned upon by the intelligentsia; some use techniques a

* Mushi no naka ni/Nete shimaitaru/Komura kana

thousand years old, others are of fairly modern development, or at least a revival and refinement. All are charming; except for one type (*bon-seki,* plates 16, 17, 18) which requires years of study and practice under a competent teacher, all may be produced in a matter of hours or days, and call for little but simple materials, an artistic eye, and reasonably deft fingers.

These miniature landscapes are divided and subdivided by the Japanese into a considerable variety of categories, over the terminology of which even the experts argue. For the sake of simplicity, and because the average hobbyist will be more interested in effect and method than in the intricacies of classical nomenclature, they will be considered here under the classifications of *bon-seki* (tray stones), *sui-seki* (water stones) and *bon-kei* (tray landscapes).

It will be observed that two of these are directly concerned with stones. It is difficult, if not impossible, for the occidental to comprehend the Japanese sentiment toward stones; not for "stone," as we feel for it in our gothic cathedrals, or even for carved stone like the wonderful lacework of the King Henry VII chapel in Westminster Abbey; but for individual stones. Why they feel as they do is lost in the mists of time and mythology. Possibly their reverence derives from prehistoric millenia of folk-memory, of a time when the inhabitants of the islands were animists or pantheists—scholars seem undecided whether it was one or the other or both. Naturally the ancient ways die out fast in the modern metropolitan centers, but in the country districts of Japan it is still not unusual to find a huge stone, girded with sacred rope, as the abode of some spirit. While the Japanese does cut and carve stone, he dislikes doing so unless driven to it. Even in building, where we would feel no compunction about cutting a stone to fit, he spends time and money looking for one which may be used without cutting. Gardens are decorated with uncut stone—one of the most famous and revered, that of Ryuanji shrine in Kyoto, consists of nothing but a broad expanse of finest creamy-colored gravel raked daily into wavelike patterns around scattered rocks. Stones are selected for shape, for color, for texture, for their ability to grow, or withstand the growth of, moss, even for their slow-drying or quick-drying property when water is sprinkled on them.

It is not surprising, then, that as we use pictures, statuettes and bric-a-brac, the Japanese brings stones into the house and enjoys them as ornaments, either alone or in combination with sand, water and plants, to produce effects evocative of mountain, sea, river and plain.

This art of stone landscape is very old, having been introduced into Japan in the sixth century, when gifts of stones were made by the Chinese court to the Empress Suiko (593-628 A.D.). At first, single stones were shown on stands or trays; later sand was added to suggest land or seascapes, and the whole art of *bon-seki* developed. Particularly fine single stones were eagerly sought after and brought (and still bring) fabulous prices. They must, of course, be "natural" stones, that is, uncut except possibly for a slight chiselling of the base to permit balance on the tray. Certain conventional symbolism arose. A stone with a greenish tinge represents the delicate verdure of spring, while a red tint represents fall. A black stone suggests the dense shadow cast by the brilliant summer sun, and a white one the snow-clad hills of winter. Particularly prized are dark stones with a white veining simulating a waterfall. Each, of course, may be shown only in its appropriate season, and carefully stored away the rest of the year.

More elaborate *bon-seki* landscapes are made by the addi-

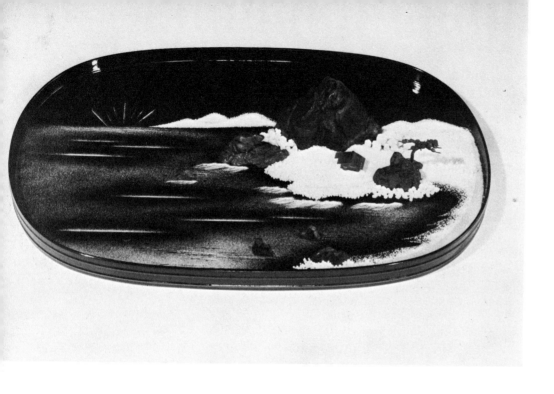

PLATE 16: *Bon-seki* ("tray stones") arranged in the style of the Hosokawa
School. Such *bon-seki* are constructed on flat trays, in a sort of bas-relief
of stones and various grades and types of white sand. Use of accessories
such as the model ships (Plate 17) and the Buddha and incense burner
(Plate 18) is a relatively new development in *bon-seki* technique

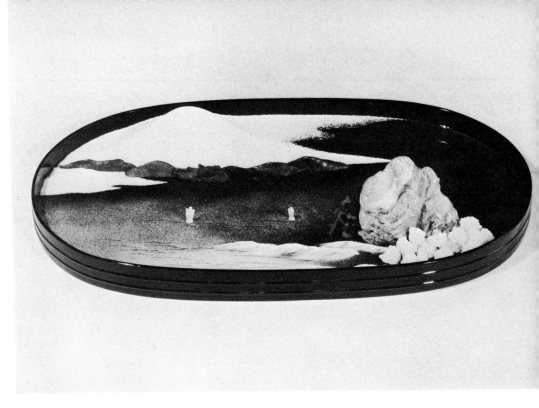

PLATE 17: *Bon-seki* ("tray stones")

PLATE 18: *Bon-seki* ("tray stones")

Dwarf Trees in the Japanese Mode

tion of accessory or auxiliary smaller stones and white sand. A tray, oblong, round or oval, with either a very low edge or no edge at all is used as a base. Black lacquer is the most acceptable material. A jagged rock in an expanse of fine, snow-white sand is a sea-girt island. Another slopes more gently down to a sandy beach, which may be boulder-strewn. Yet a third, rising in rounded steps or tiers, will, with powdery white sand "flowing" down it, represent rapids or a waterfall (Plates 16, 17 18).

From this, it seems but a step to the addition of real water with stones, and *sui-seki* develops. It is, as its name suggests, just a stone set in a dish of water; it is also an islet in a sun-flecked lake, a great cliff rising starkly from the ocean. Certain types of stones are particularly susceptible to the growth of moss and lichen, and if one of these is used, careful watering will, after a period of time, produce a patina of living green and an aura of great peace. Tradition requires that this life be produced by nothing but age and water. But one may cheat a little, by finding a stone on which moss has already started, or planting moss in the fissures and crevices of a rock of suitable shape and watering occasionally. Ordinary tap water may be used, but natural spring, river or pond water will give better results. Sometimes sand is banked around the base of the rock, to look like a beach, or the whole bottom of the dish may be covered. If the rock has a sizable depression, this may be filled with water, and turn into a mountain lake.

The dish must, of course, be of some material impervious to water. Occasionally bronze is used, but white or pale cream porcelain or glazed pottery is generally preferred, as the moss-grown stone shows up better against the lighter base. In Japan there are stores which cater to *bon-seki* and *sui-seki* artists, and dishes and stones of practically any style or design may be purchased or ordered. The American will have to hunt his own, which is more fun anyway.

And if, unversed in this cultural and traditional symbolism, one does not greatly appreciate a stone upon a tray, which frankly is very apt to look like a misplaced door-stop, the next development, the addition of tiny plants, grasses and models, can result in very charming three-dimensional living pictures—that is *bon-kei* (Plates 19 and 20).

The simpler *bon-kei* is often nearly indistinguishable in appearance from *bon-seki,* but there is a world of difference in their preparation. The structure of *bon-seki* is rigidly prescribed, that of *bon-kei* has few hard and fast rules. In *bon-seki* a stone mountain is the focal point, in *bon-kei* the landscape is limited only by the maker's imagination. Flat or rolling, hill or forest or meadow, desert or hamlet or sea or river or lake, whatever the keynote, the theme can grow and develop and take on complexity as one goes along. Construction may be completed in a day or two; or one may spend years, adding, subtracting, altering, as the whim appeals. *Bon-seki* permits of no materials save natural uncut rock, stone, sand or gravel. The elements of *bon-kei* are modeled from clay, peat, papier-mâché or plaster, then painted the appropriate color; and while real twigs, moss and grasses are used, it is not out of place to combine models with them, or simply paint them in. Real objects and facsimiles are equally appropriate. A lake may be a piece of mirror, blue-tinted glass, or a clay dish with tiny live fish. (At last one finds a practical use for guppies; they are just about the right scale!) Houses, temples, fishing boats, bridges, people, all have their places.

Whether these tray landscapes are modern or traditional seems a matter of point of view, or at least opinion. If modern, they originated with a group of 20th century artists. If traditional, they are a development of the centuries-old *hako-niwa* (box garden, garden in a box) of popular taste, which they closely resemble. The Japanese aristocrat did not care greatly for these *hako-niwa,* probably because some of the elements were manufactured, not natural; or because they left too little to the imagination. This did not, apparently, much perturb the "lower orders." In the confines of a wooden box about two feet by three, the farmer and the city bourgeois could have his garden, in fact a whole countryside, without sacrificing precious fields or living space.

The ancient *hako-niwa* were made in shallow boxes, first of wood, later of cement, and kept outside the window or at one end of the verandah; the modern *bon-kei* artist (for *bon-kei* is today acknowledged to be an art) uses trays of metal, pottery, lacquer, porcelain or stone, as well as wood, and brings his landscapes indoors. The *bon-kei* technique is excellently adapted to modern American living, for it may be small enough to live in the window of a bed-sitting room, large enough to grace a ranch house patio. The writer, who lives in a city apartment, has for the past two years derived considerable enjoyment from an Arizona desert scene—a shallow box with over a dozen different varieties of dwarf cacti and succulents in its sandy wastes. It was even inhabited for some months by a live chameleon, who seemed impervious to and unperturbed by cactus spines and was a convincing, but harmless, understudy for the desert "monsters"—and also involved construction of a cage of fine netting about 12 inches high and large enough to cover the whole box. Nor is the Americanization of *bon-kei* against precedent. At a *bon-kei* exhibit in pre-war Tokyo, one of the most noteworthy specimens was a Dutch scene, of fields, dikes and canals, complete with windmill.*

Before starting work it is necessary to decide whether the landscape is to be a temporary ornament only, or a more or less permanent structure, for these considerations affect both size and materials. The strict *bon-kei* style is intended to last for only days or weeks, while the *hako-niwa* were often kept for years. On the average, the landscape should be not less than 18 inches nor more than three feet in its longest dimension. Too small a one involves scaling so minute as to render small objects practically invisible or disproportionately large; whereas too

* Exhibit at Ueno Fine Art Gallery, Tokyo, Japan, April, 1939; sponsored by the Shizanryu group of *bon-kei* artists

large a one, such as might be planned for permanent installation on patio or terrace, is likely to cease to be a miniature and develop merely into a small-scale garden.

The shape of the container is at the discretion of the artist. Conservative taste dictates oblong or oval, but round, square, diamond-shaped or eccentric forms give opportunity for unique and characterful landscaping. The inside depth should be from one to three inches.

The amount of drainage provided depends upon the expected life of the landscape and the plantings used. For complete safety, an arrangement such as that described earlier for dwarf trees should be followed, with drainage holes and layers of gravel. However, a layer of gravel mixed with charcoal is sufficient if watering is to be light. Upper layers should be of good rich soil mixed with sand; or simply the "potting soil" one can buy by the bag at the dime store or market.

Now comes the really interesting part, the construction of the landscape itself, with its hills and valleys and ridges and rivers and plain. Let us take, for instance, a scene with a craggy mountain range descending to rolling hills in the background; a waterfall tumbles from one precipice, flows widening to the sea. Two or three houses cluster on the shore, and a footpath leads across a bridge to a tree-shaded temple. In the foreground a couple of sail boats are making for the jetty near the village.

The crags may be formed of natural rock or modelled of clay or papier-mâché and painted in tones of gray, brown and dull green. The waterfall is also painted in. If the cliffs are stone or hard clay, some of the crevices may be packed with earth, so seeds can be planted to produce real verdure. The rest of the landscape area, as far as the seashore, is covered with soil, heaped up for rolling hills, scooped out for the river bed. The river and sea may be made of fine white sand with a beach of yellow sand, or of papier-mâché painted blue flecked and streaked with white, with, of course, a rippled surface to suggest flowing water and wavelets. However, it is possible and, if the miniature is to be fairly permanent, quite worthwhile, for the hobbyist to have the river-sea formation made out of clay, pottery or metal, so as to hold real water and tiny fish. With the number of do-it-yourself hobby shops and home workshops that exist today, this should not be impossible, and adds charm to the scene. It would also be possible to substitute a real waterfall for the painted cascade, or install a mill and

PLATE 19: *Bon-kei* ("tray landscapes") made of stones, clay, sand, etc., planted with shrubs, and completed with models of people and structures. The stands on which they are placed are natural bamboo lashed with twine. The vague pattern of the background is from the gold-leaf screen against which they are shown.

PLATE 20: *Bon-kei* ("tray landscapes")

wheel turned by flowing water, through the use of an electric contrivance now on the market. Whether this would inject too great an atmosphere of mechanistic technology into what is essentially a natural art, is for the hobbyist to decide for himself.

As has already been noted, the outstanding features of the landscape may be formed of natural rock, clay, or papier-mâché. (This last is made by the method, familiar in kindergartens, of soaking finely shredded newspaper in a very thin paste, squeezing out the excess moisture, modelling the object, and allowing it to dry, then painting it.) Of the three materials, rock is the most successful if real plantings are to be made on the "hillsides," since this is impervious to the moisture necessary to keep the plants and grasses alive. If a suitable rock is hard to find, or if the hobbyist wants to build his own landscape, modelling clay is a good substitute, for if thoroughly dried and painted, it will withstand water damage. Papier-mâché is the least suitable for planting, as it rather rapidly becomes soggy. However, it is quite sturdy enough if the actual "mountain" itself is to be left bare.

The rolling hills, already formed of earth, may be covered

with moss, which, carefully watered, soon takes root and grows luxuriantly. Indeed, the whole "land" area may be covered with moss, to keep it fresh and green. The larger trees may be living twigs, which stay green a surprisingly long time if kept moist, or real seedlings, which last even longer. The Japanese like spruce, bamboo grasses, and pine; quite convincing forests may be grown from ordinary grass seed, mustard seed, even flower seeds such as marigold, though these last have a way of outgrowing their setting and have to be replaced. The amount of moisture required depends in large part on the depth of the soil. Seeds planted in the shallow soil packed in the crevices of a rock require considerable water, both to provide food and to keep the roots from drying out. Utmost care must be taken in watering, or the earth will be dislodged—an ordinary clothes sprinkler, lightly used, is an excellent watering can.

The final touch to the *bon-kei,* that brings the whole thing to life, is the little figures. More and more of these tiny models are being imported from Japan, and though genuinely appropriate or attractive ones may require diligent search among a plethora of trash, they can be found. Or again, the deft-fingered can make their own from modelling clay or papier-mâché. An artist friend of the writer specialized for a while in papier-mâché models, but papier-mâché of a highly superior type. She used not ordinary newsprint, but paper of the handkerchief tissue quality, shredded fine and soaked in thin paste. This made an exceptionally smooth, pulp-like substance, much better suited to miniature work than the coarser paper. Each tiny object was carefully built up in layers, allowed to dry thoroughly, painted with water colors, then, to give it a high gloss, "shellacked" with several coats of colorless nail lacquer. The exquisite little figures had the pristine delicacy of the earth when the world was new. That ultimate effect could be achieved, of course, only by a genuine artist—but the method is simple enough.

16

The Stranger of the Forest
(A bon-sai legend)*

TWILIGHT was deepening into dusk, the gray, cheerless dusk of a gray, cheerless day, when the traveller reined his horse before the hut at the edge of the woods. It would, he thought, offer very little shelter on a wet night. Moisture dripped from the sodden thatch, and the torn paper at the windows fluttered in the wind. Still, it would be at least a little better than lying on the rain-soaked ground under a tree; and neither he nor his horse could go much further tonight.

Dismounting, he was about to call out, when a slight feminine figure appeared at the door of the hut, and a gentle

* The following legend is included here because of the part dwarf trees play in the plot, and the insight it gives into the Japanese feeling for them. The date of the story is not known, but the reference to the Regent, rather than the Shogun, as ruler, suggests that it belongs to the period of the ascendancy of the Hojo family, who ruled in that capacity during the thirteenth and part of the fourteenth centuries.

voice, having bidden him good evening, invited him to enter the humble house. The soft tone and cultured speech struck him as being oddly at variance with the surroundings. But he made no comment, simply inclined his head, expressing, with equal courtesy, appreciation for the welcome, and asking if there were some shed where he and his beast might shelter for the night.

"We have no shed, only this cottage." The woman spoke quietly, with apology but without shame. "Perhaps your horse could shelter under the eaves. As for yourself, my husband will return soon from his work as a wood cutter, and would, I know, be glad to offer you yourself the hospitality of our home for the night. It is poor, but at least will keep the rain off. And there is no other house for some miles."

Willingly, the traveller accepted the invitation, and the woman, having fanned the gray embers in the center of the single room, was making tea for her guest when her husband entered, and added his welcome to hers.

During the meal which the woman prepared, and the conversation which followed, the traveller grew more and more puzzled. The food had been pitifully scant; the pottery rough, the chopsticks plain wood. Yet it was served with almost courtly grace, and the language of the woodman and his wife was cultured.

The night grew late as they talked. The drizzle of rain continued, and the raw cold could not be kept at bay by the scant fire the hostess fed carefully, one stick at a time, from a tiny stack in the corner. Small as it was, it did not last long. The traveller saw the woman glance at her husband, caught an almost imperceptible nod, and she went out, to return presently with a tiny tree in her hands.

At the sight of the tree, the traveller's eyes widened. It was a miniature pine, scarcely a foot high, gnarled and aged, its roots moss-covered, its trunk twisted, in perfect replica of the centuries-old giants of the forest. It was the sort of tree which could belong only to very cultured, very aristocratic, very old families, a tree handed down from father to son as a precious heirloom. Then, before he could stop her, before, even, he realized her intention, she had placed it on the fire.

The traveller turned to his host. "You will, I hope, pardon my curiosity. Your home is poor; yet your manners, your speech, are those of the court. And that tree—that can have come only from a knightly family. Yet you burn it. Who are you? What are you? And why do you burn your tree?"

Pretending not to see her husband's gesture for silence, the old lady spoke. "You are right, sir. My husband is indeed a knight, the head of his clan. His brother, by treachery, stole his castle, his estate, even his followers. And we had to flee, saving nothing except the miniature trees, which he loved, as had his father and grandfather before him. As for the pine— what is it, actually, but a tree, which will serve to keep a guest warm on a cold night?"

"But—the law—justice—the Regent-" the traveller exclaimed. "Would they do nothing? Have they heard your story?"

The old man sighed sadly. "The law? Justice? The Regent? In your travels, then, have you not seen how the country is torn and beggared by strife among the nobles? What care they for law, if they can advance their own cause? As for the Regent—does a destitute knight approach the Regent?"

The traveller nodded in regretful agreement, and as the night lengthened, the three spoke of their unhappy country, the hidden and helpless Emperor, while the fire sputtered and flamed, fed first with the pine, then with an equally perfect miniature cherry, and finally with the loveliest tree of all, a plum.

In the morning the traveller rode away, and only after he had gone did the old couple realize they had learned neither his name nor his rank.

The moon grew full and waned again twice after that, when one day word came that the Regent had summoned all knights to the capital at Kyoto. The old lady implored her husband not to go. Think how the knights, how his brother, would laugh at him when he appeared at the capital in his tattered clothes, mounted on a bony nag borrowed from a woodman friend; without armor, without squire, with no crest but the silken banner she had saved when they had fled from their home? But the old samurai insisted. His lord has summoned him, and he must go.

As his wife had prophesied, he did feel out of place in the capital, amid the fluttering silks, the gay pennons, the shining armor. He could not avoid hearing some of the comments of the other knights, and their pages made no effort to hide their amused contempt. He was sitting alone in the farthest corner of the knights' enclosure on the third morning, half wishing he had listened to his wife and stayed home, when a young equerry, even more gaily clad than any he had yet seen, came up to him and bowed deeply.

"Sir, my master, the Regent, wishes you to wait on him."

The old man looked up, suspecting some trick or cruel practical joke. But there was no derision, only a certain bewilderment in the young man's eyes. To the old man's objection that he must surely be mistaken, he explained that the Regent had bidden him bring the most poorly-equipped knight in the assembly, and surely it must be he! With formal courtesy, the equerry guided him to the center of the enclosure, where was a pavilion, the most colorful, the most brilliant, the most jewel-like of all the rich silken tents on the field. Above it flew the golden banner of the Regent.

Not daring to raise his eyes to the majestic figure on the dais, the old knight knelt humbly, but a voice bade him rise, while a page stepped forward to assist him. At the voice, the old man gasped, involuntarily looked up—into the eyes of the stranger of the forest!

The Regent, for it was he, smiled sadly. "Yes, my loyal

friend, it was I—travelling disguised through the country, that I might see for myself the true condition of my people. I found many abuses, much poverty, much tyranny—and much gentleness, such as yours. Come then, re-assume the honors of which your treacherous brother robbed you. Henceforth you, and all the oppressed, will find protection and justice at my hands."

He motioned, and pages came forward, bearing clothing and armor and weapons, and three perfect dwarf trees—a pine, a cherry, and a plum.